The Secrets of
Relaxation

The Secrets of
Relaxation

A 3-Way Program that Really Works

MARIANE KOHLER

PHOTOGRAPHS BY HENRI ELWING

STEIN AND DAY/ *Publishers*/ New York

First published in the United States of America in 1970
Copyright © 1969 by Mariane Kohler
Translation copyright © 1970 by Stein and Day, Incorporated
Library of Congress Catalog Card No. 71-122419
All rights reserved
Designed by Bernard Schleifer
Stein and Day/*Publishers*/7 East 48 Street, NewYork, N.Y. 10017
SBN 8128-1336-7

Contents

Rest is the master of movement.
       —LAO-TZUE

Introduction

What exactly do we mean by relaxation?

Basically, relaxation is a kind of exercise, but one that demands imagination and concentration.

Do you find that you can't keep your attention on things? You don't know how to concentrate? Proper relaxation will help you. A form of psychotherapy as well as an exercise, it works, through the body, on the mind.

Who needs relaxation?

Everyone needs to relax—especially worried people, anxious people, nervous people, and those suffering from stress or fatigue.

This book was written by a woman and was originally intended only for women. But the exercises can be practiced just as easily by men or children.

A man can do all the exercises in relaxation, controlled breathing, or yoga in the book. But if he doesn't like the more physical ones, he can concentrate on Chapters Six and Seven, which deal with control of the mind, and feel content in the knowledge that he is learning to concentrate his attention on his sensory perceptions.

Children should not attempt those exercises that demand too much immobility or concentration. Children can, however, easily be persuaded to try "active" relaxation—especially if it is presented to them in the guise of a game (e.g., Chapter One, Test 1; Chapter Three; and eventually Chapters Four, Nine, Ten, and Eleven).

What benefits do you get from relaxation?

You will find that you sleep better, if you suffer from insomnia.

You will develop a "conscious" repose, if you are anxious, overworked, and fatigued.

You will discover a remedy for psychosomatic trouble, for there are many maladies due simply to a permanent state of tension.

Above all, you will develop mastery of your own self, of your inner being, particularly if you lack control of, and confidence in, yourself.

Don't be content just to read this book; it is no more than a working tool. You have to do the exercises to reap the benefits. And don't be worried by the word "exercise." From the second or third lesson, you will find that relaxation is the opposite of an effort—it's a "non-do" and a "non-act," a technique that will allow you in the quickest way to achieve the deepest peace.

There is only one true kind of relaxation—but you can reach it by different routes.

First you will learn how to contract a muscle—and how to "decontract" it—in such a way as to localize, and then drive out, your tensions. A second stage will teach you how to relax by using only your imagination. A third brings you repose simply by breathing.

The book ends with a variety of exercises in hatha-yoga. They will teach you how to wake up and tone up your muscles, and how to employ your energy better.

True yoga is practiced in a state of relaxation, and is indeed the ultimate end of all authentic relaxation.

PART ONE

CHAPTER ONE

Are You as Relaxed as You Should Be? Try These Simple Tests

Eight simple exercises, all of which concentrate on the body, make up the first test. Do them slowly, without forcing yourself.

If you can do them all without difficulty, you have kept your body youthful; in your everyday life you can take the stairs two at a time, run without getting winded, sit down easily on the ground, stretch out comfortably on a hard surface. You're bothered by a minimum of tensions, mental or physical.

If, on the other hand, these exercises seem difficult, you have allowed yourself to go to seed.

Such "seediness" shows itself in the joints, which have lost their flexibility, and in the muscles, which have lost their elasticity. A muscle that has lost its elasticity is shorter than a muscle with normal tone—and that is why you can no longer do some of the exercises.

Don't give up hope, though. A body that's gone to seed can easily be restored to its former condition. You will be surprised how quickly it can be done, too—provided you take it easy and don't try to do it all at once. Begin, every day, with a quarter of an hour's relaxation. Keep this up for two weeks, and then follow it with fifteen minutes daily of yoga. You will soon find that those muscles have regained their lost elasticity—and that you can score ten out of ten on our test.

Even when you score well, go on doing the exercises once a week; they will keep you in shape. Here is the first test.

Test 1
1) Can you reach an object placed two feet above you simply by standing on tiptoe?

2) While standing, can you pick up a small object from the ground without bending your knees?

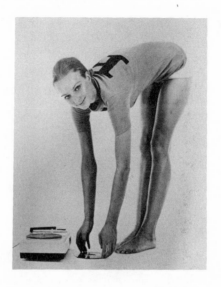

3) Can you sit on a couch with one leg tucked under you?

4) Can you sit on your heels with your toes bent to brace the feet?

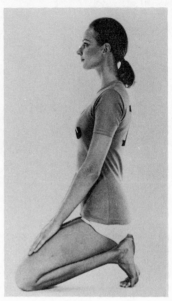

5) Can you sit on your heels with your feet stretched out?

6) Can you sit on your heels as in No. 5, lean forward, and touch the ground with your forehead—without raising your buttocks from your heels?

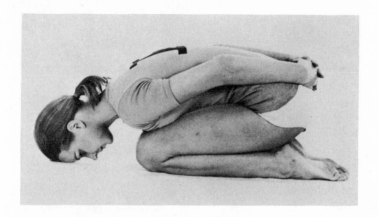

7) Can you sit cross-legged, with your feet tucked under you?

8) And then get up again without touching the ground?

The second test is designed to evaluate your reactions to stress and measure your mastery over your feelings. It comprises twenty questions, each to be answered by a plain "Yes" or "No."

Test 2

1) Do you wake up tired?

2) Do you suffer from occasional lapses of memory?

3) Are you clumsy? Do you blunder into pieces of furniture or drop things?

4) Do you slam doors?

5) Do you carry on muttered conversations with yourself in the street?

6) Do you try to get served ahead of your turn in a store? (Would you rather forget the whole thing or go somewhere else than be patient?)

7) Are you dissatisfied with your lot?

8) Does an insult upset you to the point of making you ill?

9) Do you lose your temper easily in a discussion?

10) Do you find it impossible to hear someone out? Do you interrupt?

11) Have you any nervous habits or "tics"? (Tense people are constantly tapping their feet, twisting their fingers, tugging at their clothes, or frowning. They grind their teeth, chew on their lips, or bite their nails. They forever cross and uncross their legs. They chain-smoke. And it's all simply a means of exteriorizing their tensions.)

12) Are you incapable of holding a sheet of paper at arm's length without its trembling?

13) Are you unable to sit in a chair without leaning against the back?

14) Do you jump at sudden noises?

15) Do you take on more jobs than you can manage, bite off more than you can chew?

16) Do you hate crowded rooms and crowded places?

17) Do "other people" get on your nerves if they're always around?

18) Do you make yourself unhappy over trivialities?

19) Do you find yourself going to bed "tired to death," even though you have not in fact done anything tiring?

20) Do you suffer from insomnia? Do you take sleeping pills?

If you answered "Yes" fifteen or more times to these questions, you are too tense mentally; you are messing up your life, living continually on your nerves.

17

If you answered "Yes" ten times: You are like a car being driven with the brakes on. Relaxation is a must for you. *You can learn to release the brakes.*

Test 3

The third test is a matter of self-knowledge. There exists a link, tenuous but real, between your consciousness of your own body and the equilibrium of your personality. *This perception, more or less complete, that you have of your physical self, this "body image," lies at the heart of the test.*

During the first six months of life a child is quite unaware of his body; he can distinguish no difference between it and the world around it. The world and the child form a single entity; an object is no more than an extension of his hand.

At around six months of age an awareness of the body's "separateness" begins. The first deliberate gesture is a tremendous discovery. It is repeated endlessly, refined, and perfected. Psychologists call this the "mirror state." It is the moment when you first realize that you are an individual, an isolated being in the midst of others. Later, at about the age of three, when you begin to scribble, you draw a roundish object closed in on itself like a sphere or an egg. This is your first image of yourself as an autonomous entity.

Later still you add arms, legs, hands; but it is only in your sixth year that the drawing approaches reality, that your "little man" resembles a human being. At six you have acquired awareness of your autonomy, of your own body.

From then on this self-image is enriched by every contact with the world around it. It never ceases to learn, to improve itself.

At ten you discover the smoothness of a pebble;

18

you are moved—moved perhaps to tears—by the caress of sand on hot skin, by the sheer happiness of throwing yourself full length on the grass, by the solidity of the earth that supports you.

Originally your sensitivity was diffuse, but now it has become concentrated in the areas of the body that psychiatrists call the "erogenous zones." These areas, acting as our instruments of relationship and fusion with the world, were established long before we had any clear awareness of our bodies—first (according to Freudian theory) came the mouth, then the sphincters, and finally the genital organs.

The more you remain aware of all the body's possibilities, the more your body image will become dynamic, enriched by every tactile, visual, and muscular facet of the sensibility underlying each of your movements.

And then at last this body image will crystallize through the eyes of another, through the first being you love, the first for whom your body becomes an object of adoration.

Each of us, then, possesses at the frontiers of consciousness an image, more or less complete, of his or her body. And it is thanks to this image that we are able to influence others, to integrate ourselves into the world around us.

But how do you match up to the image? Are you happy within yourself?

The man or woman who is fully at home in his or her body is like a splendid animal exactly fitting its skin; every movement becomes a pure expression of the personality.

Beauty is said to be skin deep, but in fact it has nothing (or nothing important) to do with actual physical appearance. A woman who is not beautiful can attract and please precisely insofar as she is "present" and not "absent," bodily.

This presence is the facet of you that others see; it is the part of you that will attract or repel them, on which they will judge you; it is the expression of a secret agreement—a connivance between "you" and "things."

But what if you are unhappy within yourself? If you are shy? Embarrassed? Full of complexes? Then you draw back from others physically as well as mentally. You have a sense of being torn apart, of a gulf being opened between you and the rest of the world. And there is also something strained—or too slack—about your movements.

A great deal of our success, or lack of it, is due to this question of being "present" or "absent," of facing confidently ahead or finding ourselves turned in on ourselves. And in either case the image we present to the world is indissolubly linked to our body schema and our self-image.

Now try this third test and see what you can find out about yourself.

Stretch out on the floor on your back, arms held away from the body, legs slightly apart, toes pointing outward.

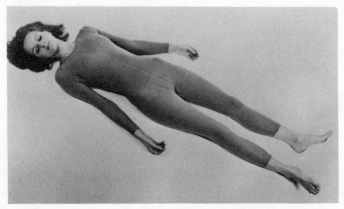

Abandon your body to the earth that supports it.

You are now in the classic position for all systems of relaxation.

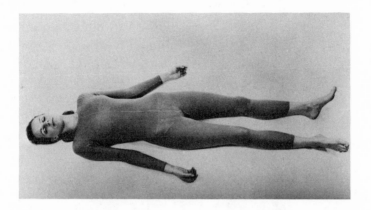

The next step is to keep silence within yourself while you travel in thought around the interior of your body.

Concentrate your attention on your hand.

Relax the muscles of your hand.

Let it lie completely inert.

Your hand seems to you to be so heavy, so *dense*, that it would require a great effort to lift it.

Repeat this exercise, concentrating successively on each part of your body. As you do it, name the parts aloud; this will help you to fix your thoughts on them.

Can I feel my right hand?

My right arm?

My left?

Can I feel my right leg?

My left?

Am I aware of my breathing?

Am I conscious of the heat of my body?

You will find that certain parts of your body *respond* to your appeal. As soon as you name them, their contours appear in your mind. You will *feel* them

21

as though your thoughts were actually inside them. You are now *aware* of them.

There will be other areas, however, that remain mute, silent, insensitive.

Now take a pencil and on the two figures outlined on this page, shade in just those parts of your body of which you are aware. Leave the rest blank.

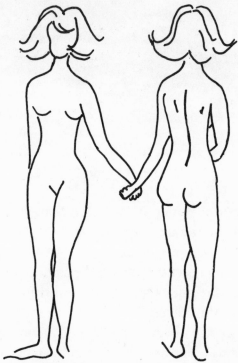

The finished drawing will show you your "sensitivity gaps"—the gaps, of course, being the white spaces. This is the image of your body as you yourself truly feel it, the picture that the body itself draws on the surface of your cortex.

If the picture shows that every zone is equally sensitive, your physical and emotional development has been effected smoothly and harmoniously. But if the silhouettes display areas of white, your psychic and physical life has suffered shocks or traumas, your emotional development has been arrested.

You will notice, too, that the blank zones, those areas where there is no sensitivity, which remain unvisited by your thoughts, are often the less-favored portions of the body; their circulation is poor, they are cold to the touch. These areas lack movement—and are thus short on tonus and muscle. They are the first parts of the body to fall victim to deposits of fatty tissue, and there is no treatment or massage that can overcome some of the more tenacious varieties of this condition.

Only relaxation in conjunction with yoga can help you to transform your body and awaken it fully.

CHAPTER TWO

A Remedy for Your Physical and Nervous Tensions

What exactly do we mean by relaxation?

We don't mean sitting on the lawn on a country weekend, doing nothing; we don't mean watching television with a glass of whiskey in your hand.

Above all, relaxation is a technique.

Sit down with your eyes closed, your right hand resting on your knee. Concentrate your attention on this hand, allowing your muscles to relax. Or, better still, when you are stretched out in bed at night, nice and warm under the covers, let your whole body go limp.

Try to become aware of *the weight of your body.*

After a few minutes you will begin to feel the weight of your tiredness, the weight of those pounds of flesh and dream and desire that we carry around every day. Flat on your back, you will discover *the key position of relaxation.* It is a position we shall use again, a position we shall perfect during the course of this book.

To concentrate one's attention upon oneself is always a fascinating experience and one that inevitably bears fruit.

Right from the start, if you happen to be gifted at this kind of exploration—or, after a few experiments, if you are not—you will discover the secret of "withdrawal." This is the key that permits you to make contact with your real self, the "you" at the center of your being.

You will also experience two sensations that will be new to you:

First, it will seem to you suddenly that it is almost impossible to move; the simple act of raising an arm will mean a tremendous effort. This is the proof that your fatigue is real; it literally has you nailed to the ground!

Second, you will feel a delicious internal warmth stealing over you. This is the proof that you are now relaxed.

You will find yourself embarked on a strange experience: You will steal away from the mental plane, on which we juggle with ideas. You will pass through—without succumbing to its blandishments—the plane of imagination, on which we play with fantasies, and you will come to earth on the sensual plane, where all is sensitivity.

For a few moments of time, you will be involved totally with your own feelings. Afterward, you can go on juggling with ideas, playing with fantasies, but you will be cleansed, regenerated, purified.

Bit by bit, you will learn to perfect this experience, to reproduce it instantly at will every time you feel the need for it.

And then, one day, you will realize that relaxation has infiltrated, as it were, all your movements. It has become a habit, a way of life, almost second nature. *For true repose lies not in the objects around us but in ourselves.*

What does "relax" really mean?

The word is of Latin origin. Literally it means to release, to let go. If a prisoner was "relaxed," he was set free.

For our purpose, relaxing means setting free the

energy that circulates within us—the energy that turns around and operates *against* us every time we become nervous or upset.

How can we explain this energy?

In repose, your muscles are constantly receiving "messages" from your nervous system, which keeps them in a state of continual slight contraction. This slight contraction is the tonus that prevents your body from collapsing in an untidy heap. It maintains the joints in their relative positions and thus defines your attitude and posture.

Tonus varies according to whether you are awake or asleep (during sleep it is at its lowest level), and according to your temperament (if you are the nervous type, your tonus is increased—you are constantly "stretched tight as a drum"). It is irregularly disposed —certain muscles are more alert than others. And it is constantly influenced and constantly changed by messages from the world outside you received by your senses and passed on by your nervous system. Parallel with these are the effects of interior changes: Each thought, every change of emotion, carries with it the possibility of a slight alteration in tonus.

This is a delicate mechanism, operated by complex nervous arrangements deployed along the spinal column, in the brain, and within the brain's envelope—the cortex.

But it is not solely a physical thing, an effect of the muscles—which is why we spoke just now of energy. Tonus is in fact a *force*, now physical, now emotional, but more often the two together.

An American physiologist, Dr. Edmund Jacobson, understood this very well when he discovered that *we also think with our muscles*. Every alteration in our thoughts translates itself into a minute contraction in

26

some part of the body. You can easily prove this yourself with a simple experiment:

Take a pendulum, or more simply a ring hanging from a piece of thread, and suspend it over a piece of paper on which you have drawn a large circle with a cross in the middle. Hold your pendulum in such a way that the weight is a couple of inches above the center of the cross—and make sure that your hand is absolutely steady. Now direct your glance, and your attention, at a point (it doesn't matter exactly where) in the middle distance.

Almost at once, you will see the pendulum begin to oscillate in the direction you have chosen.

Your hand has translated and materialized your thought—even though you haven't the slightest recollection of deliberately having imparted the least movement to the pendulum.

The fact that we think with our muscles, as indicated by the experiment with the pendulum, carries a whole range of practical applications. Once we understand that we are literally at one with our thoughts, we can control our emotional states.

In moments of euphoria, our body is completely free of tension. Is it because the muscles are relaxed, without strain, at such times that we feel ourselves happy? As soon as we become preoccupied, strained, or uneasy, we react at once with another series of contractions.

If your thoughts are light and full of goodwill, nothing but good can come of them; but if they are heavy, obsessive, negative, they will manifest themselves in a continual contraction of the muscles. And the muscles, in their turn, will act upon the organs nearest to them—which is why you suffer so often from

27

intestinal trouble, constipation, or headaches when you are thwarted.

We have said that relaxation is a technique. Relaxation is also a pleasure.

You will soon discover that relaxation brings us those rare moments, those privileged moments, when there is no disassociation between yourself and the world.

Relaxation is the consciousness of the body's movements, together with its songs, its silences, and the constant dialogue we have with it.

Three Basic Lessons in Relaxation: Learn to Release the Brakes

Imagine a car running with its brakes on. Imagine the disproportionate effort imposed on the engine, the premature wearing out of its moving parts.

You are living with the brakes on when you suffer a strained and nervous life. The engine is your body, the brakes your conscious and unconscious tensions.

Before anything else, then, you must learn to release those brakes.

If you want to yawn, yawn.

If you feel like stretching, stretch until you're sick of it.

If you feel the need to lie down on the floor, to put your feet on the table, to burst out laughing, to sing—do it.

But while you are doing it, *watch yourself*.

You will discover that you use your muscles in two opposing ways: *partly to further, partly to curb, your movements*.

A natural movement is always balanced, harmonious. *But as soon as you restrict it, you create tension and constraint*. It becomes, in fact, an antimovement. And when the antimovement becomes a habit, the tension becomes permanent, too. This kind of habit makes us sink our heads between our shoulders, stoop, clench our fists, or tighten our jaws. Let's learn to track down these negative tensions, these antimovements.

To start with, sit down, move some object, pick up a glass—and ask yourself:

Which muscles have I just used?

Why does the use of certain muscles involve the action of others?

Why do I contract my shoulder when my hand writes?

Why do I grasp my glass with so much force?

What is the *minimum* amount of force needed to hold a glass without letting it slip from my fingers?

Watch yourself carefully.

And during this initial stage resist the temptation to correct anything wrong you think you have found in your attitudes. Be content simply to make the experiment and try to relate the effort to the need.

You will discover that, throughout the day, you are using twice—or ten times—as much energy as you need.

Here are several ways to develop the sensitivity of your body.

1) Place a variety of small objects on the floor, avoiding anything fragile, pointed, or with sharp edges.

Take off your shoes.

Tie a handkerchief or scarf over your eyes (just as you did for blindman's buff as a child) and set off, barefoot, to explore the floor.

To start with, you will find that you need your eyes to keep your balance. Because you customarily wear shoes and are guided by your sight and hearing, your sensitivity to the ground and your equilibrium have in part atrophied.

But if you persevere several days with this exercise you will find that you acquire a new sense of balance—and one that owes nothing to sight or to hearing.

As for the objects on the floor, that's another experiment. Explore them with your foot, feel them with your toes, try to recognize them by their shape and their contours.

2) Try a change of tempo in your everyday life.

We have established a certain unvarying tempo for every movement we accomplish mechanically, without thinking.

Try to slow down this tempo.

Carry out a given movement twice, or three times, more slowly than usual. You may be exasperated at first, but later you will become increasingly interested as you progress and master the experiment.

3) Close your eyes and as slowly as possible, describe in space, with your arms, the dial of a large clock.

The exercise should last about three minutes.

You will feel the fluttering of your muscles, and you will have the sensation of moving your arms in a zigzag—when in fact they are moving smoothly and continuously.

4) Stretch one half of your body.

Lie on the ground with your eyes closed and your right arm stretched above your head. Now stretch your whole body, from fingertips to toes, but on the right side only (your left arm is resting at your side).

In a short time you will have the sensation that you have grown, but on the right side only.

This experiment is also a test: It proves to what degree you can modify the sensitivity of your body by the power of your imagination.

What is the goal of these exercises?

To make you discover for yourself that your muscles rarely work in synchronization. Some of them will have the normal tonus, as much in action as in repose. Others are too strained and do not know how to slacken off. Others are dulled and do not know how to awaken themselves. You can find this out for yourself by feeling your muscles or studying yourself in a mirror.

A muscle that is too strained, or suffering too much tension, is hard. A muscle that has atrophied is flaccid; it tends to become enveloped in fat. A muscle with the normal amount of tonus is firm and elastic; it burns up the fat around it.

You will find out also that you waste your energy: There is always more tension than you need in your body. And finally you will discover that an unnecessary amount of tension persists in your muscles even when they are at rest.

The purpose of these tests is to prepare you for your first lesson in relaxation.

In this first lesson, you will learn to release the brakes, to slacken off the strongest of your tensions.

1) *The Woodcutter*

Are you familiar with the woodcutter's movements when he is splitting logs?

Imitate him. With your legs apart, your feet firmly planted on the ground, straighten up to your full height with your arms above your head—and then let yourself fall forward from the waist with all your weight, just as though you were wielding an imaginary ax.

2) *The Tree*

Let your arms dangle, trying to make them as heavy as possible.

Incline your head.

Bend gently at the knee.

Now fold forward accordionwise on yourself, and sink to the floor like a falling tree—or like a garment that slips from its hanger.

3) *The Leaf*

Hop up and down in place, on one foot.

But instead of keeping your body rigid, extend your other leg to the rear, allow your torso, head, and arms to fall forward, and let them all flop, bounce, and swing to the rhythm of your hops.

4) *The Washing*

Now imagine that you are a piece of washing hanging on the line in the sun.

You are standing up, legs apart, feet firmly on the ground.

Now lean forward from the waist, letting your head, shoulders, and arms all hang loose—as though you were hanging folded over an imaginary clothesline. Let the wind gently stir you from right to left, blow you up and down.

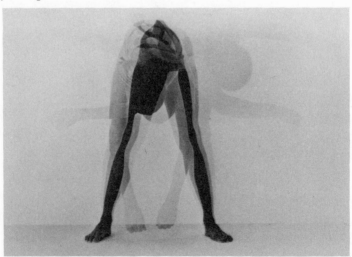

5) *Relaxing the nape of the neck*

Does your face look strained? Do you suddenly look your age?

Try this remedial exercise.

First, allow your head to fall forward onto your chest; then, to make the relaxation really efficient, half-open your mouth and let your chin fall. After a few minutes, you will feel a natural traction drawing the nape of your neck. Under this pulling effect, the muscles of the nape will yield little by little, and your neck will stretch.

Afterward, practice this exercise for improving the carriage of the head:

Straighten your head, stretch your neck, and draw in your chin until you feel a slight discomfort behind the ears. This is the position in which your head should be; it is a mistake either to poke it forward, as though it were dragged by the weight of your jaw, or to straighten it artificially by lifting your chin and compressing the nape of your neck. Finding the right position is a matter of trial and error.

You can now finish off your first lesson in relaxation with one or the other of the following exercises:

6) *Relaxing the face*

To slacken the facial muscles and minimize wrinkles, place your fingers and thumbs on your scalp and draw backward, firmly but gently.

After thirty seconds, let go. Your face will resume its natural expression, but it will no longer be strained.

Open your mouth wide—as wide as if you were trying to swallow an apple whole. Poke out your tongue. Open your eyes as wide as you can.

After ten seconds, return to normal. (It's not pretty, but it works!)

7) *Relaxing the scalp*

Take a small lock of hair between your fingers and thumb, and pull it with a series of quick, small tugs. Work over your whole head in this way, lock by lock, inch by inch, until you have covered the entire scalp.

With your head bent forward, apply your fingers, slightly separated, at the level of your temples. Start to massage your scalp with your fingertips, working in small circular movements and moving toward the crown of your head.

To relax the nape of your neck, press your two thumbs above your ears, swivel your other fingers backward, and massage with them as before, always working toward the crown. The friction should be light to start with and gradually get stronger and stronger.

An additional advantage of this massage is that it improves the health of the hair by stimulating circulation in the scalp.

8) *Relaxing the hands*

Imagine that you have rinsed your hands in water. Shake them vigorously, as though you wanted to get rid of the drops of moisture.

A variation is to take the index finger of your left hand between the forefinger and thumb of the right, and then shake your left hand, which should be completely limp. Repeat with the other hand.

9) *Relaxing the feet*

For a woman, a pretty foot is narrow, slim, lean, muscled, and at the same time vigorous and relaxed. Much the same can be said for a man. How can you achieve strong, relaxed feet?

First, a massage. Massage your feet completely with olive oil. Take each toe separately and massage that. Stretch the toes. Rotate each toe separately.

Exercises. Standing up, try to pick up an object with your foot—a big pencil, a large wad of paper, a small ball of yarn. To grasp the object, you must clench your toes.

Sit down on the floor with your legs stretched out in front of you and with your feet about twelve inches apart. Contract your toes as in the previous exercise, and, without moving either your knees or ankles, try to bring one big toe near enough to the other to touch it.

Rotate each ankle clockwise and then counterclockwise.

Standing up, shake each foot rapidly (as you have already done with your hands—see page 36).

Kneipp's bath. Walk barefoot on damp, dewy grass, on the beach at the water's edge, in a stream, in a small pool warmed by the sun—or even in a bathtub ankle-deep in cold water.*

The ritual Japanese bath. The Japanese husband never brings his office worries and the fatigues of the day home with him. The Japanese relaxing bath is the "open sesame" that works the trick.

Before coming home, the dutiful husband plunges himself in the *furo* to release himself from his toxins and his tensions.

In Japan, this bath is given in a small, individual swimming pool, but in your home you can make do with an ordinary tub:

a) Scrub yourself under the shower with soap and a sponge to remove all impurities.

b) Rub your body briskly—paying special attention to the back and the legs—with two handfuls of

---

* At every step you take wearing shoes, your foot automatically expands and contracts. When it expands, its length increases by about three-eighths of an inch. It is imperative that you buy shoes big enough to allow for this expansion, big enough to permit your foot to move freely. This means that there should be a gap between the tip of the toe and the end of the shoe of at least three-eighths of an inch. You can really test a shoe only by walking in it.

mineral salt (coarse sea salt, for example) with which you have mixed a teaspoonful of essence of lavender.

c) Plunge into a bathful of hot water (about 104° F.) to which you have added two handfuls of coarse sea salt. Add more hot water—as hot as you can possibly take it—and lie there for ten minutes.

d) To keep from getting thirsty, suck slices of fresh lemon.

e) Get out of the bath, pat yourself dry, and then cover your body with perfumed oil. Massage lightly so that the oil will penetrate your pores. (In Japan you would be massaged at length by a kinestherapist.)

f) Stretch out in a warm, shady spot, with a cover over you. You will find yourself relaxing and often you will fall asleep.

g) When you wake up, refresh yourself with a cup of jasmine tea.

Time-saving formula for a relaxing bath. Cold water is stimulating; hot water is relaxing. If you're pressed for time, therefore, run a little hot water into your tub, sit down in it, splash it all over your body, and scrub yourself with a good brush.

Finish off with a very hot shower, letting the water fall on the nape of your neck and run down your back.

CHAPTER FOUR

Learn to Stretch

Have you ever watched a cat wake up?

It's fast asleep—or seems to be. Its whole body is relaxed.

Then it opens an eye.

It puts out one paw.

It stretches.

It yawns, uncoils itself, and stretches its whole body. It seems to get longer and longer, like a rubber band.

Imitate the cat.

Lie down on the floor and stretch yourself as much as you can, from your fingertips to your toes.*

And then let yourself go limp.

You will relish the sensation of complete repose.

This is true relaxation, this fleeting pleasure you feel immediately after stretching.

You have stretched your muscles, extended them, in the same way that you might stretch a spring. The muscles—like the spring—return to their normal position once the pressure is released. Your body is calm, and this feeling pervades your brain, too.

We have said, though, that the experience is fleeting. Why?

---

* Don't make the mistake of having someone else help you to stretch. Someone else may pull too hard and tear a muscle. You don't run this risk when you do it yourself; your body knows what it's doing and controls its own movements.

Because you have experienced it in a passive state —and real relaxation is active.

You must learn to stretch your muscles—but you must learn also to prolong and deepen the resulting state of calm.

The restfulness you promote in this way will extend to the muscles of the brain, and the brain will relay it to the other organs of the body. Your whole being—body, mind, senses, memory—will fall into a kind of half sleep.

Lie down on the floor and get someone to mark, with chalk or a piece of string, the precise length you occupy on the ground.

Then suck in your stomach, stretch the nape of your neck, extend your arms and legs—and once again stretch your whole body, voluptuously, from the tips of your fingers to the tips of your toes.

When you've finished, have your body length measured again.

You will find that it is from one to two inches longer than before.

What has happened?

Your muscles have for a few moments regained their "real" alignment.

The spinal column is made up of vertebrae that cannot stretch by themselves. But each vertebra sits on a small cushion of flexible tissues that separates it from its neighbor and acts as a shock absorber. When you stretch, your vertebrae separate, the cushions swell, increase in volume, and finally regain their elasticity.

Now try another experiment. Measure your waist before and after stretching.

You will discover a strange thing: The inch or so that you have gained in length you have lost in girth.

You have become thinner; your abdomen has been sucked in.

Naturally, as soon as you are on your feet again, your silhouette will shorten and thicken—the body will resume its bad habits.

But if you practice relaxation and yoga with a certain amount of persistence, this temporary state can be transformed into a permanent one. Your muscles will become longer; your body will rediscover its youthfulness and its flexibility.

The "analytical" relaxation of Edmund Jacobson (the man who discovered that we also think with our muscles) operates on the principle of the spring. When you pull on a spring and then let go, it returns to the position it was in before it was pulled. In the same way, when you stretch muscles and then release them, they will return to their position of relaxation without any further action on your part.*

This kind of relaxation is termed "analytical" because it proceeds little by little, one segment at a time.

You tense one set of muscles and then release them; you repeat this three or four times with different sets—and each time the relief is more noticeable.

But why, you may ask, should I stiffen and contract myself, when you say I am already too stiff and strained?

The answer is simple: because there is a very big difference between contracting the muscles voluntarily, deliberately, and contracting them unconsciously. When you contract your muscles involuntarily, you are the victim of badly directed energy and you are thus a prisoner of your own muscle contractions.

* This is a physical or "progressive" method, as opposed to the psychic or "global" method you will learn about in Chapter Four.

But when you contract your muscles voluntarily, you are making a conscious exercise of will, and one that will help you relax.

All the following exercises are to be performed lying on your back on the floor or on a firm exercise mat. Your body should be as free of strain as possible, your arms slightly out from your sides, your legs slightly apart, your toes pointing outward.

Your eyes should be closed. When you close your eyes, you suppress to a certain degree your relationship with the outside world, and it is thus easier for you to concentrate on your movements.

1) *Relaxing the arms*

Bend your right arm across your chest.

Close your fist.

Tighten your fist as much as possible, then open your hand.

Allow your arm to fall back to your side.

Notice your sensations. The first time you do this exercise, you'll hardly feel any difference. But when you have repeated it three or four times, lengthening the period of rest in between each repetition, you will notice the disappearance of all tenseness in your arm. Then you will be able to concentrate on releasing all the tiny tensions that remain.

Practice the same exercise, using your left arm. When you have achieved a satisfactory absence of tension in both arms, go on to the next exercise.

2) *Relaxing the legs*

Bring your legs together, and press them tightly against each other.

Draw back your toes.

Push down on your heels, as if you were trying to make yourself longer.

The muscles of your feet, ankles, calves, and thighs are now strongly contracted.

Keep up the pressure for several minutes, and then release it.

Allow your legs to fall back into the position of rest, slightly parted, with your toes pointing outward.

As in the preceding exercise, do it over again until you feel that you have obtained a satisfactory "decontraction." Afterward, as before—and always in that position of rest, with your arms slightly apart from your body and your legs slightly parted—you can concentrate on removing any small, remaining tensions.

3) *Relaxing the thorax*

Still stretched out on the floor, breathe in deeply to expand your chest.

Hold your breath for three seconds.

Breathe out, expelling the air slowly through your nose.

The muscles of your rib cage, having been tensed, now relax, and your chest flattens.

4) *Relaxing the abdomen*

Still lying on your back on the floor, breathe out and at the same time suck in your stomach as though you were trying to attach your stomach wall to your backbone, and your backbone to the floor.

Hold this position for three seconds.

Then allow your stomach to return to its normal position and the air to refill your lungs naturally, without forcing your breathing.

5) *Relaxing the back*

Lying on the floor as before, hollow your back and try to bring your shoulder blades together.

Your back is thus lifted off the floor.

While you are in this position, press down with

the back of your head, your arms, the small of your back.

After a few moments of this tension, allow your body to return to the normal position.

These first exercises have allowed you to locate and identify feelings of tension within you—and to discover their opposites: relaxation, release, the art of letting go.

You have noted the difference between a muscle that is stretched and one that is relaxed.

You have also found that there are certain resistances: Some muscles seem more difficult to relax than others. These are the muscles in which the tonus is at the highest level, or those most often used (the leg muscles for the runner, those of the right arm for the fencer, those of the shoulders, the arms, and the wrists for a typist).

Certain resistances, too, can have a mental origin. If you are the nervous type, your shoulders, thorax, and stomach are likely to be tense.

But in any case, the stage we have reached is only an intermediate one.

When you really know the difference between tension and relaxation, it will become unnecessary for you to create tension in yourself deliberately just so that you can relax.

The exercises in relaxation that we have done should always be followed by several minutes of total rest, lying on your back, with your arms held slightly away from your body.

Never fall into the error of believing that you can relax, in the sense that we mean, simply by staying still.

True relaxation means precisely the opposite. It comes from movement, but movement from within.

When you are relaxed, your body is stretched out

limp as a rag. Your mouth is half open, your eyes are half closed, and the lines on your face have smoothed out. Your breathing is slow and deep.

If you are simply imitating this state of relaxation —if you are faking it, in other words— you'll achieve nothing better than a counterfeit copy of the real thing. Your face will remain strained, your eyelids will blink furtively, and your body will betray small starts and jumps all over.

When you begin genuinely to unwind, you will find you have an irresistible urge to yawn. Be glad when you do because this is a sure sign that you are on the road to real relaxation. Yawning expresses a longing for more air that you have been stifling—perhaps for years. The more you relax, the stronger your desire to yawn will be.

You will know that you are really relaxed when you find you have a temporary inability to move. The smallest, simplest gesture—moving your hand, for instance—seems almost too much of an effort to contemplate.

You must never, on any account, pull yourself abruptly out of this state of relaxation.

Remember that you are not a single homogeneous whole; rather, you are made up of many layers of personality, each representing a different "you."

The first layer is your surface personality—the one that other people see, the one whose image is so essential to your life. You use this surface "you" in public. If anything happens to surprise the public you (an unexpected noise, the doorbell), you react without any difficulty and are capable of handling the situation.

Beneath this surface, though, there exists a second self. This is your "dream personality"—the "you" of the sleeping or daydreaming state. If something jolts you out of either of these states, you still react without too much distress: The bridge between the "dreaming you" and the "surface you" is quite short.

But the "deep you" is way beyond these states. The "deep you" is the self of dreamless sleep—and of profound relaxation.

Any call from the outside world, when you are plunged in your "deep" state, can provoke a shock— and this is why you should never, under any circumstances, drag yourself abruptly out of a state of relaxation.

Take time to float slowly back to the surface.

Stretch yourself to tone up your muscles.

Yawn, breathe deeply, open your eyes and close them again, stretch once more.

Finally, get slowly to your feet.

Slowly, for you have been diving deeply into your inner self, and you need a few moments of transition before you emerge once more into the air.

CHAPTER FIVE

Learn to Rest

"To rest, to stretch, to sleep, to die, with one's
back to the ground . . ."
—Le Corbusier,
Poème de l'angle droit

When it comes to relaxation, the Orientals are the masters, and the most perfect techniques of all come from the East.

After having discovered Edmund Jacobson's active and "analytical" relaxation, I experimented in "global" relaxation under the direction of Madame Jordhana, an Indonesian adept.

Madame Jordhana asked me to stretch out on my back on the ground, my head supported by a little cushion at the nape of the neck. "If you like to keep your head high, that is," she told me. "Or, if not, in any position you find comfortable."

She leaned toward me, lifted my right arm until it was a few inches from the floor, shook it slightly, and allowed it to fall back to the ground.

She did the same thing to my other arm, and then to both my legs.

Thus I found myself rather in the position of a puppet that has been tossed on the floor, or even (though it is a comparison I do not like) of a dead body. My feet were apart, my arms lay slightly out to

47

the side, and the backs of my hands rested on the floor with my fingers curled lightly against the palms.

Madame Jordhana made me realize that this position of total rest *called for no effort*—true repose is essentially non-acting and non-doing.

When I was thus relaxed, the electromyograph (an apparatus that measures tension in the muscles) registered no residual tension at all, the only remaining contraction in my body being a "tonus of repose," which would diminish as time went on.

Relaxation, therefore, works on two planes: on muscular tension, by suppressing every unnecessary movement; and on the tonus, by allowing it to subside to its lowest possible level.

Madame Jordhana next asked me to concentrate on those parts of my body that happened to be in contact with the ground. In a low, persuasive voice (though I must confess this seemed a trifle superfluous to me), she proceeded to enumerate them: the back of the head, the shoulders, the forearms and the backs of the hands, the shoulder blades, the buttocks, and finally the calves and the heels.

She explained to me then that our bodies are traversed by currents of energy. These start, she said, from a point situated just about an inch below the navel and end at the crown of the head, the toes, and the fingertips.

"Never mind," said Madame Jordhana, "if this idea runs contrary to all you have learned in your anatomy classes: In the East, this concept is part of a science that is thousands of years old. For the moment, accept it, and ask no questions."

She then asked me to travel, in thought, slowly along these energy routes that she had mapped out, starting with my right arm.

48

For ten minutes I concentrated hard on doing this. What I was doing, in effect, was to feel my arm *from the inside*—and then, successively, the other parts of my body, in which energy seemed to flow back and forth.

I felt myself pervaded by a sensation of well-being. Within a few moments, consciousness of my fingers, my hands, my wrists, had almost faded away.

My spirit floated unattached, without desire, in a state that was almost beatific.

During our second meeting, Madame Jordhana didn't ask me to stretch out on the floor, but simply directed me to a chair. When I had sat down, she drew my attention to the fact that my body could be divided vertically into two halves, front and back.

The front half comprises the five senses, the stomach, the feet (which carry us forward), the hands (which capture and seize), and, in short, all those parts of the body by means of which we maintain contact with the world.

The back half comprises nothing but elements of support—the shoulders, the back, the spinal column, the buttocks.

"Like most women," she said, "you are always hurling yourself forward; you are always straining toward something, always ready to grasp something. Your eyes seek for images to capture; your ears are listening for sounds.

"Learn to draw back, to use the support of your own spinal column, and, instead of leaning forward to seize things, let things come to you.

"Your head should always be in a position of equilibrium at the top of your spinal column—it may seem silly to say this, but it rarely is in such a position. It is dragged forward by the weight of the jaw, or held

49

artificially upright by contracting the muscles of the neck.

"It's a waste of energy to try to compensate for these bad habits because there is one position in which the head is truly balanced and blooms like a flower at the end of its stalk."

"But how do I find this one position?" I asked.

"You stretch the nape of your neck," she said.

"You tuck in your chin—to the point where the action provokes a feeling of discomfort behind the ears.

"You close your eyes, and you try to perceive, from within, this sensation of complete equilibrium.

"And it's no good at all trying to check your position in the mirror: You can succeed only through intense concentration."

Madame Jordhana also explained that every emotion, each little mental difficulty, is reflected in a contraction in some part of the body. She distinguished two separate kinds of contraction: those deriving from something wrong and those produced by my ill-directed efforts to right whatever it was that was wrong.

"By doing this," she pointed out, "all you do is accentuate your disequilibrium by piling one contraction upon another."

At the beginning of the third lesson, I stretched out once more on the floor.

"Let your weight *fall!*" Madame Jordhana told me.

"Feel the heaviness of your head, of your trunk, of your limbs, as though they were trying to dig themselves into the earth, and remember that you are wasting energy every moment by *carrying* the weight of your body, when in fact it would be enough to allow this weight to drop, to commit it to the ground, whether you are standing up, seated, or lying down."

In fact I did feel the weight of my body—a load

so heavy that I realized, for the first time in my life, that I had spent forty years of my existence dragging it about needlessly.

"Now," Madame Jordhana continued, "imagine that you are an island. Your breasts thrust up from the ground, like dunes. Your hand is a coastline indented by deep bays. Every part of your body that touches the ground grows roots that penetrate to the center of the earth.

"You are an island at the mercy of the tides. Feel how the waves hurl themselves at the shore.

"Concentrate now on your breath. Breathe quietly without in any way altering your normal rhythm."

I concentrated on my breath.

It became quieter and quieter, and the quieter it got, the deeper it became.

It seemed to me that I was breathing with my stomach. It was an extraordinary sensation.

After a few minutes, it seemed that I wasn't breathing at all—*but that I was being breathed.*

We tend to live always on the surface; our attention is forever claimed by what is going on *outside* us.

Following Madame Jordhana's guidance and doing these exercises, I learned to deflect my attention away from its usual preoccupations and channel it toward the interior of my body. In doing so, I found a strange sense of well-being: the sensation of returning to the source of my being, of listening to the very wellspring of my existence, of being at rest at the still center of the turning world.

We have found that there exist three routes of approach to "active" relaxation.

By means of the first (Chapter Three), we learned to slacken off the stronger tensions.

By means of the second (Chapter Four) , we found that a muscle operates on the principle of the spring: If you put a strain on a muscle, and then let it go, it returns to its original position—but "untensioned."

The third route (which I learned from Madame Jordhana) is subtler: Relaxation is achieved by means of images of relaxation itself. The teacher appeals to the imagination of the student, to the student's power of autosuggestion.

This Hindu method inspired the "autogenous-training" system perfected by a German psychiatrist, Professor Schulz. Schulz, who has lived for the past twenty years in France, is primarily a hypnotist. He has found that under hypnosis there occurs a kind of "disconnection": The links between a man and his brain are partially severed. This phenomenon is accompanied by a double sensation of weight and heat.

Schulz has discovered that not only are these two sensations corollaries of hypnosis, but they contribute, in some measure, to the creation of the hypnotic state itself.

He who experiences them necessarily effects a cerebral disconnection: *He cuts himself off from himself.* He detaches himself from his own body—just as we do every night in the few minutes before we fall asleep.

Autogenous training must take place in a warm, quiet, half-dark room. Try it.

Stretch out on your back on the floor, with a small pillow at the nape of your neck, another under the small of your back, and a third behind your knees. Close your eyes to help cut yourself off from the outside world.

Then roll your head from left to right (without lifting it from the floor) to relax the muscles at the nape of your neck.

Next, allow the weight of your body to fall. Imagine that it is sinking like a root into the earth.

Now concentrate (if you are right-handed), on your right arm.

Try to *feel* its weight. (You'll do it more easily if you remember that your arm weighs about one-twelfth of your total body weight—ten pounds if you weigh 120.)

To help yourself, repeat mentally five times: "My arm is heavy. It is becoming heavier and heavier. . . ."

(Autogenous training consists, essentially, of maintaining *active autosuggestion*.)

Your right arm is now heavy, so heavy that it might be glued to the ground.

Now repeat the process for the left arm, trying to make this arm, too, as heavy as possible, repeating mentally five times, "My left arm is heavy. It is becoming heavier and heavier. . . ."

When both your arms seem to weigh a ton, turn your attention to your right leg. "My right leg is heavy. It is becoming heavier and heavier. . . ."

And then do the same with your left leg.

The first stage of the process, then, is an awareness of *weight*. The second stage leads you to an awareness of *warmth*.

When your right arm is heavy and relaxed, your blood vessels become dilated. Your circulation becomes more active. A wave of heat passes over your body.

You didn't feel it the first time?

That is because you were not paying sufficient attention. Repeat the experiment (right arm, left arm, right leg, left leg) but this time concentrate on the sensation of heat.

"My right arm is warm. It is getting warmer and warmer. . . ."

(Naturally, you can't hope to succeed the first time: You must keep trying for several days—or even several weeks.)

Actually, the sensation of heat is not a result of autosuggestion. The heat really exists—though you are not yet sufficiently well trained to perceive it.

Each time you achieve true relaxation, a wave of heat will pass over your extremities. Schulz actually measured it with a thermometer.

This fact was graphically illustrated a few years ago in Germany, when a team of mountain climbers was buried by an avalanche. After two hours, the trapped men were reached. All of them were injured, their hands and feet frostbitten—all except one, that is, and he was one of Schulz's students! During the two hours he was under the snow he had practiced his "de-contraction" exercises, stimulating his circulation and thus maintaining his body temperature.

When these sensations of weight and heat have become thoroughly familiar, you can begin to practice "global relaxation."

All you have to do is stretch yourself out on the floor and let your weight fall. You are then able to draw on all the resources of your imagination.

Imagine, for example, that your body has no more substance than a parachute that is about to land on the earth; it billows out, slackens, flattens itself—and then becomes one with the ground.

Or imagine that you are the branch of a tree that breaks, falls, and then buries itself in the soft earth.

Better still, think of yourself as one of the millions of tiny plankton floating on the surface of the sea, rising and falling at the will of the waves. This last image has the added advantage of drawing your attention to your breathing. When you are relaxed, your breathing is slow and deep—very similar, in fact, to the breathing of a person who is asleep.

During the 1920's the theory of autosuggestion postulated by the French psychotherapist Émile Coué was very popular. Coué's method involved the use of a certain number of key phrases, which in time were anchored in the subconscious and became conditioned reflexes; whatever action or state the phrases described became habitual. Schulz has perfected this system.

In this connection, it is instructive to recall the story of another German, Dr. Hannes Lindemann, who wished to study the problems of survival at sea, and therefore decided to cross the Atlantic alone in a canoe hollowed out of the trunk of a tree.

During a storm, on the thirty-sixth day of his odyssey, he lost his rudder. Then, suddenly, he saw a passing ship, and frantically signaled for help. He shouted and screamed, but in the storm nobody saw him or heard his cries. The unfortunate Lindemann fell prey to fear and despair.

Eventually, however, he arrived at his goal.

Two years later he repeated the experiment. But this time, under Schulz's direction, he went into training and established a kind of "mental conditioning" beforehand. At the end of every autogenous-training session, he mentally repeated the four phrases:

I shall go on to the end.
I shall head west.
I will not give up.
I won't accept help from anybody.

Once again, Lindemann was caught in a terrible storm, complete with whales, sharks, and mountainous waves. Once again a ship crossed his course. But this time the lone sailor's unconscious was forewarned and forearmed. He succeeded in his self-imposed task without accepting help from anyone—and this time without experiencing panic or despair.

You too can profit from his experience.

When you are stretched out in a condition of true relaxation, your inner self is open to any suggestion, providing always that it comes from you.

When you are in this state, sow a few suggestions in your mind like seeds. They will flourish and bear fruit. To make certain that they work, though, it is essential that the suggestions be stated as impersonally as possible. For example, if you want to give up smoking, don't say: "As soon as such-and-such a thing is over, I shall stop smoking." Say instead: "It doesn't matter to me if I smoke or not." Repeat this slowly, several times, like a litany.

If you love someone who doesn't reciprocate your affection, you can use the same routine. Don't say: "From now on it's all over between us. I won't think about him anymore." Simply say: "I couldn't care less about him."

You can use your state of relaxation equally well to prepare yourself for some future action. This is a technique frequently used by athletes. During their autogenous-training sessions, they are taught to live through, mentally, the event for which they are being prepared in advance, to imagine and analyze every possible movement they may be required to make.

If you must steel yourself for an important interview or some other difficult situation, try to imagine the whole scene in advance. Go over it mentally, step by step. Work out what you are going to say. Think of all the questions you may have to answer—and of the most impressive way of replying to them.

CHAPTER SIX

Breathing—the Key to Self-Control

Nothing reveals your inner state as much as your breathing.

Are you in good health, happy, and thoroughly in control of yourself? Then your breathing is deep, slow, and rhythmic.

Are you the nervous type? In that case, your breathing is rapid and shallow.

Are you anxious? Worried? You gasp and catch your breath.

If you are irritable, your breathing is irregular and nonrhythmic.

Your breathing can even tell an experienced observer whether you are from the country or a city dweller. The clean, fresh air of the fields, the mountains, or the sea stimulates the respiratory function. Country people therefore are deep breathers. On the other hand, city air, which is always polluted, has the reverse effect: Instead of breathing in great lungfuls of it, the city dweller holds himself back. He uses no more than a quarter or a fifth of his lung capacity each time he inhales.*

* Certain cells in our respiratory apparatus are furnished with fringes like tiny eyelashes that beat the air in such a way as to promote a more intimate mixture of the oxygen and the blood. It has been established that these lashlike fringes beat five times less quickly in contact with city air than they do when the air breathed is from the country.

Besides differences in city and country air, there are differences in ways of breathing.

Bad breathers inhale harshly, while sucking in their stomachs, raising their shoulders, and thickening their necks.

Good breathers start by *exhaling*—with their stomachs held in. When they have let out all the air they can, and their lungs are almost empty, their bodies naturally demand more. The diaphragm acts like a simple pump; the stomach swells, and the air rushes in again—without any effort on their part!

Good breathing is full, deep, and slow. It has a rhythm of its own and is unaffected (or very little affected) by emotional changes.

In correct breathing of this kind, the diaphragm plays an essential role. A membrane swelling slightly at its upper end, the diaphragm divides the body in two, separating the chest from the abdominal cavity.

When we inhale, the diaphragm creates suction, rather in the manner of a syringe, and this in turn provokes a need for air at the base of the lungs. The diaphragm exerts a light pressure on the organs it covers—the liver, the stomach, part of the intestines, the spleen—and effects a continuous, gentle massage on the contents of the stomach.

When we exhale, the diaphragm returns to its former position and thus helps the lungs to empty themselves of air.

As each breath is drawn, the stomach therefore swells out slightly under the pressure of the diaphragm —to return, on the exhalation of breath, to its original position. This undulating movement can be seen best in animals and babies.

Let us now learn how to breathe well.

1) *Natural breathing*

58

You are stretched out on the ground in your customary position of relaxation (feet slightly apart, arms away from the body, toes pointing outward, palms of the hands facing the ceiling). Lying like this, you are in the best position for the fullest possible expansion of the rib cage. Your chest, ribs, and shoulders are completely relaxed.

All you have to do is let yourself breathe as simply as a sleeping child—but this is by no means as easy as it sounds.

Try to imagine that there is a small cork floating on your navel, rising and falling absolutely evenly with the movement of the waves. But breathing is a difficult function to observe, because no sooner have you fixed your attention on it than your very concentration disturbs the rhythm.

The answer is to use that form of attention that is almost inattention, which remarks without regarding, which passes over things without dwelling on them, a variety, in fact, of "interior vigilance."

2) *Abdominal breathing*

Still in the same position, breathe in through the nose with a slight whistling sound. Your stomach will swell.

Concentrate on "feeling" the air. The most sensitive part of your nose is less than half an inch inside the nostril.

Follow the course of the air as it passes through your nose to your throat and larynx, finally penetrating to your lungs.

Once your lungs are full, hold your breath for a moment.

Then breathe out again through your nose, closing your mouth firmly. Your stomach will automatically be sucked in as you do so.

This kind of abdominal breathing should be practiced all the time, in all weathers, standing up, sitting down, or in bed, just as soon as you have mastered it.

Abdominal breathing has these advantages:

(a) It acts continuously upon the diaphragm, thus effecting a constant massage of the viscera.

(b) It is the only one among our so-called vegetative functions (that is to say, those concerned with growth) that we can control—and in controlling it, we also control our impulses and our psyche.

(c) It acts upon the sympathetic nervous system and thus helps to regulate and steady all the "natural" functions of the body.

3) *Total breathing*

Total breathing is breathing with balance, super-breathing. You can do it several times a day, *but never more than twice in a row*, and always preceded by a few minutes of abdominal breathing.

Inhalation and exhalation are both effected in three stages. Lie down in your usual position of relaxation. Exhale normally. And then:

Stage 1: Breathe in as though you were getting ready for a deep sigh. Breathe through your nose, with your mouth closed, distending the stomach (this first stage is similar to abdominal breathing).

Stage 2: Your rib cage expands.

Stage 3: Your collarbones rise. Hold in the resulting lungful of air (apnea), for about five seconds (the time it takes to count up to five mentally).

Now, exhale, still breathing through your nose, with your mouth closed.

Stage 4: The collarbones subside.

Stage 5: The ribs follow suit.

Stage 6: The diaphragm returns to its normal position and the stomach flattens out again. Once this has occurred, stay like that, with empty lungs (dyspnea), for another five seconds, before starting again to breathe normally.

Later on, you can prolong the periods when your lungs are full or empty, for up to sixteen seconds—but the two must always be exactly equal in length. The exercise can be said to be a success when you feel a sensation of well-being after it. It can be said to have failed if, when your lungs are empty, you have a sensation of suffocation.

Total breathing has all the advantages of abdominal respiration, plus these added benefits:

(a) It completely aerates the lungs (each breath inhaled by a normal person brings on the average a pint of fresh air to the lungs; but deep breathing increases this amount dramatically to between three and four pints.

(b) Holding the breath increases the surface of mucous membrane in the lung exposed to the fresh air. The blood, better oxygenated, thus exercises a tonic action on the organs it serves, and this in turn helps to conquer fatigue.

(c) In the lung, holding the breath creates first a superpressure then an absence of pressure. The lung thus works at its maximum power.

4) *Alternate breathing*

Sit cross-legged, or on your heels, or even on a chair—it doesn't matter too much, so long as you keep your back absolutely straight.

Your body should be flexible, your spinal column supple, your head so lightly balanced that it almost seems to be suspended from the ceiling by a wire. The nape of your neck should be stretched and your chin drawn slightly in.

Place your right thumb on your right nostril, your

right index and middle fingers against your forehead, and the ring finger of your right hand, bent down for the purpose, against your left nostril.

With your thumb, press against your right nostril so that the passage is closed.

Breathe in slowly, deeply, through your left nostril.

Now press your ring finger against your left nostril, closing that passage too, and release the pressure of your thumb against your right nostril.

Breathe out through your right nostril.

Start the process again, this time breathing *in* through your right nostril, and *out* through your left nostril.

Continue until you have completed the exercise seven times. Remember, though, that this exercise must not be attempted more than twice in any one day.

The advantages of alternate breathing are:

(a) It acts like a sedative on the nervous system.

(b) It forces you to breathe very slowly—and this in turn results in a gradual and uniform unfolding of the inner cells of the lungs.

5) *"Dead-leaf" breathing*

This is a system of complete breathing associated with a technique of relaxation.

Kneel down on the floor with your toes stretched out behind you. Sit back on your heels. Breathe out, slightly sucking in your stomach.

Still on your knees, raise your thighs, torso, and arms to a vertical position, stretching up as high as you can. Breathe in.

Sink back onto your heels—but this time bend your torso forward, stretch your arms out before you, and allow your head to lie between them. Breathe out and rest for a few moments in this position.

CHAPTER SEVEN

Living at Ease

1) *How to rest the mind*

When you are relaxed, stretched out on your back with your thoughts free to wander, a succession of images will pass through your mind. Only now the rhythm is different: The images come more slowly, and you have time to observe them.

Try not to make your mind a total blank, because that is virtually impossible, but do try to slow the rhythm of your thoughts still further.

Become a spectator and watch the workings of your own mind.

When an image crosses the field of your consciousness, act as though you were a viewer in front of a television set or a movie screen. Let the image cross your private "screen," dwindle, and vanish, without trying to name it, identify it, or bring it into sharper focus with the aid of your memory or your imagination.

You can switch your attention from these images to concentrate it on a sensation felt by your body itself. (This is actually what you have already done, in your apprenticeship to relaxation, by concentrating on letting your weight fall—only this time you are going to do it systematically.)

Patiently fix your attention on your breathing—or on the point of contact between your back and the floor.

You will find this demands a particular *kind* of concentration. Your attention must be fixed on the object of the exercise, yet it must be neither strained nor even active (a strained concentration is analogous to a muscle under contraction); it must constitute vigilance without tension.

In such a state, you are genuinely receptive—open to any or all the sensations that present themselves to you. Try, then, to be voluntarily receptive to:

The first sound that impinges on your ear.

Immediately after that, to the various smells in the room in which you are lying.

Then to the contact between your hand and the floor on which it lies.

And, after several seconds, to your own breathing.

This whole exercise should not last more than a minute—but during this minute you have, several times, been totally absorbed in a single sensation. Mental fatigue, however, derives from the fact that you customarily and continuously mix the sensations that you receive—the thoughts, the associations of ideas, the fantasies that occupy your mind. Stop this continuous blending. Confine yourself to single, pure sensations—and you will automatically set your mind at rest.

Such pauses are extraordinarily beneficial. They suspend the eternal round, the relentless progression of your thoughts; they put you, literally, in direct contact with the "real" world around you; and they induce in you the concentration that is essential if you wish to become the master of your thoughts.

Education of the brain begins with control of the simplest movements—opening a door, crossing the street, picking up a knife. It is not necessary to control all your actions; you simply do it, every time you think of it.

Try this experiment the next time you are at the dentist's. If you have to have some minor treatment without an anesthetic, concentrate on relaxing. The moment you begin to feel tense, take a deep, deep breath. And hold it. (This is the principle behind "natural" childbirth—the patient is so preoccupied by her breathing, by controlling her muscles, that she has literally no time for suffering.)

A further example: Headaches, nine times out of ten, are the result of prolonged contraction of the muscles of the nape of the neck. The tension in these muscles exerts pressure on the blood vessels, which consequently cease to carry the full amount of blood necessary for the proper functioning of the brain.

The remedy is exercises in active relaxation, scalp massage (Chapter Four), breathing exercises (Chapter Six), and yoga (once you have learned what to do).

Every time you find yourself prey to sudden fatigue, or feel nervous tension mounting, take time out to "get into yourself." It's quite easy to do. Simply take some object and stroke it with your fingertips, allowing the sensation it brings to penetrate the core of your being. (Orientals, whose calm is legendary, habitually carry with them a string of amber beads which they "tell" between their fingers; this sensory contact serves as an outlet for their tensions.) Each time that you manage to switch all of your attention in this way onto a single object, the relaxation it brings spreads, like a spot on a sheet of blotting paper, through your whole body.

Naturally, you cannot expect to succeed with these exercises all at once. And there will be many times when you will forget about them altogether in the rush of everyday life.

That's why you have to make sure that you do

them at opportune moments. Self-mastery can be learned, but training is necessary.

One day, the sudden knowledge will come that you have won your battle. You have become capable of enduring maximum tension without being disturbed.

Relaxation has become a part of you.

2) *How to rest the eyes*

"I put an apple on the table," wrote Henri Michaux. "Then I put myself into the apple. There's peace for you!"

An odd experiment? Let's try it for ourselves.

You put an apple on the table (or a flower, or anything that pleases you).

Then sit down.

And finally prepare, with a deep sigh to put you in a proper state of relaxation, to enter into communion with, or contemplate, the apple or flower. There are three ways in which this can be done, but only the last one is of any value.

In the first, which unfortunately is the most common, our gaze only skims over the object. We look at it without really seeing it. Its image never reaches the conscious part of our brain.

In the second, we do pay attention to the object. We seize it, fix it between our two optical axes, examine it, mentally dissect it. There is a whole vocabulary describing the manner in which this can be done. We look at the thing "with wide-open eyes"; we "devour it with our gaze"; we "glue our eyes to it"; we stare at it "searchingly" (all of these expressions imply vigilance or tension).

But to enter into the apple and become one with it—that's something else again!

I do not attempt to seize the object. I let it come to me (or, more exactly, we meet halfway).

68

After several minutes—if you think of it this way and if you are sufficiently gifted—something will happen. All at once this apple will seem more beautiful. Its colors will appear more brilliant, its form more exciting. And you yourself will find that you are happier, calmer, more relaxed.

Then you will have the feeling of being in communion with, of making yourself one with, the object you have chosen.

And now that you know you have succeeded, and the experiment has paid off, there is nothing to stop you repeating it—not just with an apple or a flower, but with a landscape, a painting, a great work of art.

Vision is the means by which the attention enters into contact with the world, and the eye is its intermediary.

But the eye plays a secondary role in the process (one can have a wonderful view and not know how to look at it). The important thing is the depth at which the contact is established.

Depth of the right degree can be acquired, even if you do not succeed the first time. It is the experiment with the apple all over again. But when you do succeed, what a revelation! Whatever it is that you are contemplating, you feel that you are seeing it for the very first time.

"Beauty is in the eye and not in the object," says an old Arab proverb, telling us that beauty will remain secret so long as we remain incapable of seeing it.

Our eye is comparable to a camera. It "takes" an image, which the optic nerve carries to the brain, where it is "developed." The image is inverted at first, but the brain elaborates it, accommodates the inversion, and finally restores to us a correct interpretation of the original image.

Therefore, we see as much with the brain as with the eye. "The eyes canalize the messages received by the visual receptor," wrote Aldous Huxley. "The mind takes possession of these materials and elaborates them to the point of the finished article, which is normal vision of exterior objects."

The eye "tunes in" on the object it perceives. For a long time it was believed that this focusing was effected solely by means of the accommodation of the eye's lens, and that both myopia (nearsightedness) and hyperopia (farsightedness) were due to a lack of elasticity in the lens. Today, however, it is known that the focusing effect is achieved, not only by an accommodation of the lens, but also by the compression or elongation of the whole eyeball.

The tiny muscles that order these movements are involuntary—we have no power to control them. But they are an extension of the larger voluntary muscles surrounding the eye that permit us to look up, down, and from side to side.

Every system of ocular exercises starts from this point: We exercise our voluntary muscles in the hope that the small involuntary muscles controlling the accommodation of the eye will automatically follow suit. However, it is enough simply to put the voluntary muscles at rest to start the others correctly practicing their work of accommodation.

The best of all relaxation exercises for the eyes is "palming"—which at the same time relaxes the whole face.

Sit down at a table.

Place your elbows on the tabletop, lean your head forward, and let your crossed fingers rest against your forehead, with the heels of your hands pressed against your cheeks beneath the eyes.

Your eyes are thus enclosed by the palms of your hands, which form two small, dark chambers around them.

Now close your eyes—and at the same time try to relax the muscles of your face.

On the dark screen formed by your eyelids, project an image—a landscape that you like, a face that you love—it doesn't really matter what it is.

Sit down at one end of a room. Run your eyes, slowly, without moving your head, around the molding of the ceiling, the angles of the walls, the floor.

Or run them over the molding around a door, the outline of a cupboard.

In the two previous exercises, your head was motionless; only your eyes moved in their sockets. Now here is one in which exactly the reverse is true:

Choose an object nine or ten feet away from you.

Turn your head, slowly, to the right, and then to the left, without ever letting the object out of sight. (This time, it's your head that moves and your eyes that remain immobile, fixed upon the object.)

Finally, in the country, or at the seaside, you can

71

easily—and most agreeably—rest your eyes by letting them dwell on the horizon.

3) *How to rest the ear*

On board *Gemini* V, astronaut Charles Conrad complained to mission control at Houston about the constant irritating noise made by a valve that clicked eternally. Mission control suggested to him that if he would just try to learn to *love* the valve, the noise would help him to sleep.

All of which means, not that we have to love the things that irritate us, but just that it pays sometimes to turn a situation upside down, to look at it from the opposite point of view.

When a disagreeable noise imposes itself on me (like Conrad's valve), I become aggressive and irritable —but passive. And as soon as I accept the fact of the noise and *listen* to it, it becomes less annoying.

That's the difference between hearing a noise and listening to it.

When I hear a noise, it imposes itself on me; but when I listen, I am consciously choosing to hear it.

If the noise is regular—like the sounds of a train in which you are traveling, or the racket of a pneumatic drill below your window—begin by listening attentively to it. See if you can find an underlying rhythm to it. When you've done that, make up a tune to go with the rhythm.

All you have to do then is sing!

And at the end of a quarter of an hour, you won't even have to do that. The song will sing itself. It will have become lodged in your brain, and it will automatically superimpose itself on the disagreeable noise.

You say that such a tune, in such a setting, runs the risk of becoming obsessive?

72

It does, of course—but surely it's better to be obsessed by a song than by an unpleasant sound.

After the palliative, the cure. Are your ears assailed by piercing noises? Are they anesthetized like those of the typist who no longer hears the clatter of her own machine?

Then they must be consciously reeducated.

When you are in a crowd, try to isolate one voice, to hear it and only it. In the country, focus all your attention on a bird's song, on the sound of a stream, or the wind in the branches. Lend your ear to these harmonies. Be "all ears."

When you are quietly alone at home, sit down. Relax. Take a crystal wineglass and a knife. Tap gently on the side of the glass to make it ring. Shut your eyes and listen. Follow the sound. Trail it like a detective until the moment when it dwindles into silence. Repeat the experiment.

At the end of a few days you will be surprised at how much more sensitive your ear has become.

Under the same conditions (in peace, alone, in silence) listen to a record you particularly like. But listen to it in a new way. Instead of listening to the whole orchestra, concentrate on, say, the violin, as though the violinist were playing just for you. Play the record over, and do the same thing with the piano, with the brass section, the flutes.

You will be amazed at the richness, the treasures that you will discover in a very short time.

PART TWO

CHAPTER EIGHT

Yoga:
Superrelaxation

Yoga is a technique that comes to us from the East, a technique that has been in existence for three thousand years. It is a complex of rules—moral, ethical, and physical—whose goal is to help man transcend the temporal envelope in which he is encased and break the barriers separating him from the infinite.

Hatha-yoga, with which the next four chapters of this book are concerned, is only one small section of yoga's grand design—that part of it dealing primarily with the body.

This form of yoga is an art in itself, the art of good health and long life. It is a form of kinestherapy perfected over the centuries by doctor-monks who practiced "natural" medicine. It seeks the remedy for the ill it treats within the body itself, at the same time requiring the body to react in a manner that can only be salutary.

Can such a technique be of any use today? Certainly it can. That is why its study and application are becoming so widespread.

In fact, it can be of very great use—providing it is not expected to be a panacea. If you suffer from some illness, if one of your organs is seriously damaged, don't launch yourself into a crash course of yoga all alone, believing or imagining that it can cure you. But—

if your trouble is fatigue

if you can't manage to control your nerves

if you are hypersensitive and superemotional

if you sleep badly

if you are getting rusty and look your age

—*then yes, emphatically, yoga is for you.*

As opposed to the classic gymnastic exercises, yoga comprises a series of movements that are slow and rigorously controlled, the body building up harmoniously toward predetermined postures, which are called "asanas."

Each asana should be a minor masterpiece in itself, and if it is achieved correctly it will have several different effects on the body.

From an external point of view, the asanas will make several sets of muscles work and help to make the joints more supple.

The postures will also have more profound effects: They will dissolve the deposits that lie at the heart of rheumatism and arthritis. They will attack both waste products and deposits of fatty tissue. They will massage the viscera, activate the bile, stimulate the intestines and the liver, and regulate the metabolism. Finally, they will act upon the internal glands secreting the different hormones whose functions are vital to your glandular balance and to the general state of your health.

Each asana comprises three separate phases:

1) You assume the posture, making your muscles work in a fashion that is slow, progressive, and continuous. This is the dynamic phase.

2) You "freeze" in the posture you have chosen. This is the static phase. For the moment, you are transformed into a statue. You remain immobile for several seconds—as long as you can before feeling uncomfortable.

3) Slowly, you return to your original position. Then, with great economy of movement, you lie flat on your back. In this position you relax your muscles, get back your breath, and embark, when you are ready, slowly, upon the next posture.

On no account should you forget the third phase of relaxation and rest. Don't neglect it, thinking the more postures you can cram into a quarter of an hour the better. This little rest is extremely important in yoga because it is during this phase—*when nothing seems to be happening*—that you store up the benefits of the asana you have just finished.

The blood is coursing through your veins, cleaning out the poisons and feeding the muscles; the fatigue generated by the exercise is immediately dissipated.

To repeat: You must never start one asana immediately after another, but always rest a little in between.

How long should you rest?

That depends on your temperament and on the state of your training.

In principle, you should remain in a position of relaxation until your heartbeat and your breathing have regained their normal rhythm.

In the East, one is taught that the rest should be the same length as the asana preceding it, and that in any case it should never be less than one minute.

There are seven good reasons why you should take up yoga.

1) *In yoga your muscles work in extension.* Bend your arm, doubling your fist and contracting your biceps (like an old-fashioned muscle-man).

The muscle fibers shorten and swell; the muscle is working in a static position. A muscle constantly working like this becomes hard, but it will lack suppleness, adaptability, and quick response.

79

In yoga postures, your muscles always work in extension, and these extensions are slow, progressive, and continuous.

A muscle working in extension becomes slender. It will react quickly, adapt itself easily, acquire finesse and force. This is why yoga is also a system that promotes beauty: It helps to mold your body, to refine it, to make your flesh firmer and your features more relaxed.

As for stretching . . . Well, you know about that anyway, don't you? It's a big treat for the muscles, something like a long, controlled yawn.

2) *In yoga your muscles work with a minimum of nervous fatigue.* Working in extension is the most economical way to exercise your body. When a muscle is contracted, all the nerve fibers are in action, which means a maximum outlay of nervous energy, and thus maximum fatigue. But when the muscle works from an extended position, as in yoga, not all the fibers are in action; the result is less muscular expenditure and nervous tension, and no fatigue.

3) *Yoga limbers up the spinal column.* As you know, the spinal column is composed of rigid vertebrae interlaced with disks of more supple material.

In hatha-yoga exercises, the spinal column is constantly stimulated, with the result that the vertebrae separate, and the disks, freed from the pressure that usually weighs on them, regain their suppleness and their elasticity. The spinal column, instead of subsiding into a slouch, lengthens—perhaps by as much as an inch.

4) *Yoga limbers up the joints.* Each posture acts upon a certain number of joints (the shoulders, the neck, the wrists, the groin, the knees, the ankles) and calls on them to function at the limit of their possibilities.

The "opening" of the joints in this way—which can actually be measured by laboratory instruments—controls the *quality* of your movements; the more flexible your joints, the more facile and flowing your movements.

In addition, every time you make your joints really work, you are helping to dissolve the toxins that can concentrate in those areas and thus produce arthritis and rheumatism.

5) *Yoga improves the circulation.* When your blood circulation is stimulated, your organs and tissues benefit from the rich blood supply and function better.

When you are in a bent posture, the liver empties itself of blood; it is in effect flushed and drained like the sump of an automobile.

When you assume a seated posture, your circulation, compressed in your legs, becomes more active in the rest of your body.

An inverted posture forces the blood toward your torso and head and thus carries a more intense flow of nourishment to the brain.

6) *Yoga will help you to concentrate.* Why will it do that?

Because the slower movement involved in yoga demands a greater effort of attention; you simply cannot carry out yoga routines mechanically, thinking of something else. To succeed with any given asana, you have, at every moment, to control the whole complex of your body and proscribe every movement that has not been reasoned and thought out.

Every movement is ordered from within you and encourages you to turn inward, upon yourself.

Your attention is thus switched from the exterior problems that preoccupy you and is brought back within the limits of your body.

And since your attention cannot be divided, it follows that if you apply yourself properly to your movements, you will therefore cancel out your worries.

Confidence in yourself begins with tranquillity, equilibrium, and the mastery of your own movements.

7) *Yoga gives you mastery over your body.* Why? Because you are continually controlling your body!

Each asana represents a balance between tension and relaxation: You tense those muscles you need to use; you relax the ones you don't. And you learn, thereby, to control your own energy.

It is essential, therefore, that the various movements be performed correctly and practiced in a predetermined order, one having as its goal the completion, or balancing, of another. There is no half yoga!

Nor is there any room in yoga for "almosts" or "not quites." Under these conditions your movements would have no more significance for you than the action of bending over to pick up a pin.

Even if you only have a tiny room there is always room for a throw rug, and for yoga that is enough. (I use a blanket spread on the carpet, working in warm, loose clothing, with—and this is important—bare feet. The best outfit is tights with a pullover.)

There's only one absolute "must," but it is imperative. *Always work in silence.*

Work alone, or with other students of yoga, but never in the presence of spectators. The presence of outsiders hinders your concentration; it tempts you to work for others and not for yourself, and it engenders the spirit of competition, which is completely alien to yoga.

Before you begin a posture, study the illustration carefully. Try to imagine yourself in the act of performing this exercise. During the dynamic phase, concentrate your attention on the technique of movement you are about to accomplish.

Take up the posture slowly, avoiding all unnecessary movement, any wavering.

During the static phase, concentrate your attention on economy of movement; release all the muscles not involved in the action. Your posture will be good when you can achieve it and hold it for some time without effort and without any unnecessary movements.

During the rest phase, concentrate your attention on your breathing.

Do your yoga exercises regularly. Ten minutes a day will prove more profitable than one hour once a week.

Don't work more than you need—and never do the same exercise more than twice in the same session. Above all, never try to force things. If you do, you run the risk of nullifying the good effects of yoga.

If you force yourself, your willpower is strained, your muscles contracted. The yoga you practice then is nothing more than a system of acrobatics—it brings neither rest nor relaxation. True yoga is exactly the opposite; it should be practiced with suppleness and ease.

Stop at once if you feel any kind of tension or contraction.

Wait a few moments.

And then, if the pain persists, abandon the exercise until the next day.

If the pain disappears (which is more likely), push yourself a bit further and try again.

But always stop yourself on the threshold of pain.

Do each exercise once only; twice is the absolute maximum.

But never, never more than twice in succession.

CHAPTER NINE

Three Basic Lessons in Yoga: A Morning Routine

Are you one of those happy people who leap out of bed at dawn, shaking the house with their zest for life as soon as they open their eyes?

Do you get through an enormous amount of work before noon (though it's true that by the end of the day you're showing signs of strain and are thankful to get back to your bed in the evening)?

Or are you the opposite type?

Does it take wild horses to drag you out of bed? Do you spend the whole morning trying to find excuses not to work?

If so, you'll be the opposite in the evening, too: you'll feel brilliant, euphoric, and you will get through an enormous amount of work then. You won't have any desire to go to bed at all; and when you do go, it will probably be as late as possible.

These behavior patterns are blueprints for two opposite temperaments: those who work well in the mornings and those who work well in the evenings.

Until recently it was thought that these characteristics were the result of habit, or temperament, or even of taste.

But we know now that your pattern depends on the rhythm of your sleep.

If your behavior falls into the first category, as soon as your head touches the pillow you slide right into a deep sleep that lasts about seventy minutes.

Then you return to a light sleep, which lasts another ten minutes.

After this, you sleep deeply again, you emerge once more, and so on. But as the night goes on, the periods of deep sleep become shorter, the periods of light sleep longer, and this light sleep conveys you naturally to the waking state.

If, on the other hand, you belong in the second category, your sleep starts off light and gets deeper and deeper as the night goes on.

It's at its deepest, therefore, when it's time to get up. And that's why you find it so difficult!

American sociologists have christened the first type of people "larks," and the second type, "owls."

What can you do if you're an owl?

Obviously, it is beyond your power to modify your sleep pattern. But you can at least learn to wake up well.

As soon as you awaken, take control of your body by performing a series of stretches. (You can do them while you're still in bed.) Stretch yourself until it hurts! Then let go and enjoy the sensation of languor you'll feel.

Next, wake up your body with a stinging tepid or cold shower and follow this with a brisk rub.

If you can't stand cold water, you can take—believe it or not—an air bath, naked, with the window open. And as soon as you feel cold, dive back into bed for a few extra moments.

Whether you're a lark or an owl, the yoga you practice in the morning is a toning-up routine.

It is composed either of stretching movements (the Cobra or the Bow), or of postures intended to stimulate the circulation, warm up the muscles, and make the joints more supple (the Half-Lotus, the Back Stretch, or the Twist).

Of course, you can do these exercises at any time

of the day—when you're tired out with mental work, or simply for the pleasure of doing them.

1) *To begin*

Always start off the session with a few minutes of relaxation (lying on your back, in the position you have learned) and abdominal breathing (see page 59).

2) *The Cobra*

This exercise takes place in two stages.

Stage one: Lie flat on your face, with your hands level with your shoulders, and your chin pressed to the ground.

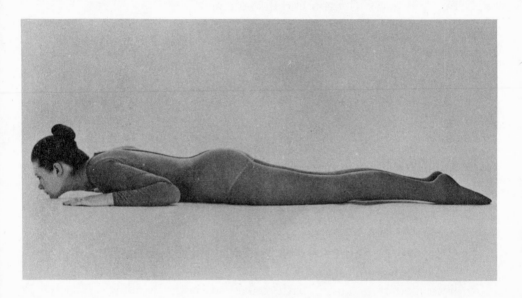

Breathe in, slowly lifting your head and pushing your chin forward.

Bend the top half of your body slowly backward, making your back hollow. (Your hands should remain in the same place, your arms slightly bent.)

Hold this position for some moments, and then lower yourself slowly back to your original posture.

Stage two: Without moving your hands from the ground, slide yourself backward, folding your body so that you are sitting on your heels.

Your back should stay flat, and your head should be as near as possible to the ground.

This double posture makes the backbone flexible, increases the expansion of the rib cage, elongates the neck muscles, and strengthens the muscles of the stomach and back. It is believed to stimulate the thyroid gland, combats constipation, and decongests the utero-ovarian complex.

3) *The Bow*

Lying face down, your chin pressed to the floor, bend your knees and grasp your ankles with your hands. Your knees should be slightly apart, your heels touching your buttocks.

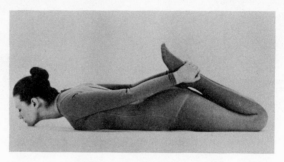

Breathe in . . . and then raise, in a single movement, your head, shoulders, and knees, separating your knees as you do so.

This movement stretches the arm and thigh muscles and expands the rib cage. It reshapes the chest, flattens the abdomen, straightens up the stance, and improves the carriage of the head. It is also believed to work on the alimentary canal and to stimulate glandular secretions.

The Cobra and the Bow are both "anti–spare tire" and "antibulge" exercises.

4) *The Half-Lotus*

Lie on your back and rest for a few minutes in the relaxation position.

Then sit up, steady and well balanced on your buttocks, with one leg bent double and the other stretched out at a slight angle.

Take the foot of the bent leg and wedge it against the opposite thigh, sole upward, as near as possible to the pelvis.

You will find that the knee of this leg has a natural tendency to rise. Try to persuade it as near to the ground as possible, with a series of small pushes from your hand.

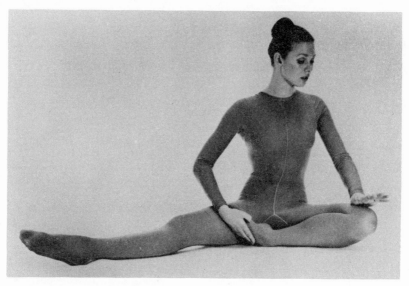

Repeat the routine with the other leg.

This movement is a preparation for the full Lotus posture. It limbers up the joints of the ankles, knees, and hips.

5) *The Back Stretch*

Put the foot of your bent leg back on the floor, but keep the leg itself still tucked up close to you.

Take a deep breath, then exhale as you lean forward to rest the top half of your body against the leg stretched out in front of you.

If it helps, you may grasp your foot or your ankle (but avoid putting any tension on your arms). It is preferable to bend your knee slightly.

Hold this position, empty-lunged, without breathing, for as long as possible, and then return to the position from which you started.

This posture stretches the back muscles and the muscles at the backs of the legs, helping to make them more supple. It combats the deposits of arthritic material that tend to form along the spinal column.

6) *The Twist*

Still sitting up, bend your right leg and cross it over your outstretched left leg, keeping your right foot beside your left leg.

Twist your torso to the right.

Press your left hand behind your left knee and your right hand, palm outward, against your back, between the shoulder blades. Repeat, changing arms and legs.

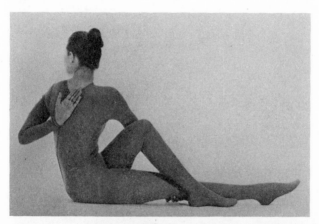

This exercise helps to make the back more flexible. It is believed to have a direct effect on the digestive functions, to facilitate peristalsis, stimulate the liver, and pep up the endocrine glands.

7) *The Diamond Mudra*

Lie down in the position of rest.

Then sit on your heels, with toes extended and back very straight.

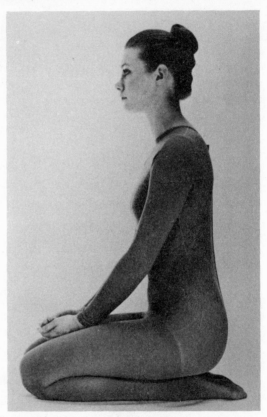

Now, lean forward, one hand grasping the other behind your back. If you're supple enough, you should be able to touch the ground with your forehead. If it's difficult, stop halfway—but in either case make sure your buttocks do not rise up off your heels.

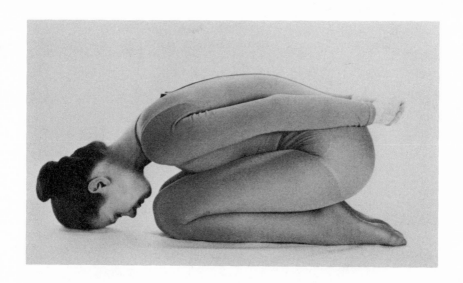

This posture stretches the dorsal muscles and those in the buttocks and at the backs of the thighs. It compresses the stomach and decreases flatulence.

CHAPTER TEN

How to Prevent Fatigue

In September, 1966, five hundred psychologists from all over the world met in Paris to exchange views on fatigue. At the end of their deliberations they decided (what we knew already from experience!) that fatigue is not an illness but a common denominator of all illnesses—a total response of the organism to the worries and difficulties besetting it.

How can we defend ourselves against fatigue?

In the best military tradition—by attacking it, preventively, on its own ground.

What are the best remedies?

Diversion (fatigue is frequently born of boredom).

Relaxation (which not only stops fatigue, but keeps it from starting).

Physical exercise (which concentrates on the muscles and is thus an antidote to intellectual and nervous fatigue).

All three of these remedies are united in yoga, which is simultaneously a diversion, a relaxation, and a physical exercise. It fights, moreover, against dispersion of mental energy (another source of fatigue) by forcing you to concentrate.

Breathe out.

Raise one leg into a vertical position, without bending your knee.

Hold it there a few seconds, and then lower it

slowly to the ground. (If this second part of the exercise seems too difficult at first, you can bend your knee before lowering your leg to the ground.)

Repeat the exercise with the other leg.
The whole thing should be done three times.
2) *The Grasshopper*
Roll over, face down, arms at your sides, fists clenched, and chin pressing against the floor.

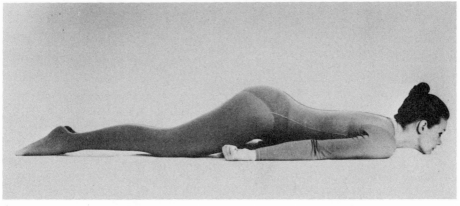

Now suck in your stomach so that no part of it touches the floor, and breathe in as you raise one leg, keeping it straight, into the air.

Breathe out.

Lower the leg.

Repeat with the other leg.

Repeat the exercise—very slowly—three times.

Both these exercises accelerate the circulation of the blood. They strengthen the abdominal wall, flatten the stomach, and trim the pelvis and thighs.

3) *The Complete Posture (or Shoulder Balance)*

Roll over once more onto your back.

Lie in the position of relaxation for a few minutes.

Then, still stretched out on your back, raise both legs to the vertical position. The legs should be held stiffly together, with no bending at the knee, and the palms of your hands should be flat against the floor.

Hold this position for a short time.

Breathe in. Breathe out.

Make sure your legs are still parallel, straight, and stretched up as far as they will go.

Now, press down on the floor with your hands and raise the lower half of your body.

Place your hands under your hips to prop yourself up.

Straighten your legs (they will tend to drop toward the rear), and extend your whole body as near as possible to a vertical position.

Force yourself up higher by progressively stretching the back—always maintaining yourself in the position you have reached with the help of your hands (don't keep your legs rigid, let them stay relaxed).

Breathe abdominally to avoid congestion of the face.

Hold this position for several seconds—or, if you can, for several minutes.

Then bend your knees, bringing them as near as possible to your face.

Stretch your arms out on the floor beside you again, palms down.

Then return slowly to the horizontal position, lowering yourself gently, unrolling vertebra by vertebra.

Keep your abdominal muscles contracted until the last moment—until your whole body is touching the floor again.

This "progressive" posture is designed to replace the standing-on-the-head position. It acts upon all the organs, which are suspended upside down and lightened.

It works wonders with the circulation, hurrying the blood on its journey back to the heart. It combats fatigue, heaviness in the legs, varicose veins, and congestion of the lower abdomen. Through the increased flow of blood to the head, it helps to abolish wrinkles, and is thought to banish worries and aid the memory.

It is one of the most important postures in yoga.

4) *The Plough*

This is a spectacular variation on the preceding posture.

Stretched out on the floor as in the previous example, raise both legs together, press palms down on the floor, and lift the lower half of your body.

But instead of stopping halfway, as in the Complete posture, push on until your legs are over your chest and head and your toes are touching the floor behind you.

Do not deliberately try to compress your chest, but try to straighten your back.

To return to your original position, bend your knees and bring them slowly down to the floor as in the Complete posture.

The Plough has the same advantages as the Complete posture: It relaxes the muscles of the stomach, the back, the shoulders, and the neck.

5) *To make the knees more flexible*

Sit down on the ground.

Bend your knees.

Lower your legs and place the soles of your feet together.

Grasp your feet with your hands and draw them toward you, while keeping your legs in a horizontal line.

Hold your back very straight.

Try, with continuous small movements, to bring your knees as close to the ground as possible.

This exercise is not a traditional posture, but it helps to make the knee joints and the thighs more flexible.

6) *The Tree*

For this exercise, you begin by standing up.

Bend your left leg at the knee and rest your foot

on your right thigh, at the same time joining your palms together and raising your arms above your head.

To complete the exercise, balance first on one leg, and then on the other.

This exercise is actually a test that demands a great deal of concentration. You'll bungle it if your attention wanders for a moment.

7) *The Pupil's Posture*

Sit down comfortably, with your weight evenly distributed on your buttocks. Bend one leg double, with the knee against the floor, and stick the other leg slightly out to the side, keeping it quite straight (avoid the temptation to bend your knee).

Your hands, palms upward, should rest on your knees.

It is possible that the knee of the bent leg may not touch the ground. Do not attempt to force it down; facility will come naturally with time.

Once you are in position, close your eyes and breathe calmly.

Concentrate.

When you've done this, change legs.

This posture, like all the seated ones, develops concentration and makes the joints of the knees and the hips more flexible.

CHAPTER ELEVEN

Yoga for the Evening . . . Yoga for Escape

Come home in the evening and retire into your shell. Draw the curtains that keep the world at bay. Your home is your private paradise, your island in the sun. Here you can safely immerse yourself after you have unshackled your chains and severed your last ties with the day.

When you go to bed, you will "sleep the sleep of the just"—*if you know how to transfer your attention from the innumerable objects claiming it to one single object*, after which it's a simple matter to cut this last thread.

Sleep is a journey toward the habits of infancy, a voyage, in a way, into the past. Curled up under your blanket, you instinctively find the movements of your childhood.

The evening yoga we recommend, therefore, is a kind of rehearsal or preview of the movements you are going to make naturally during the night anyway. Look, for example, at the images the postures suggest: the Egg, in which you are folded in upon yourself, like a chick in its shell; the Oyster, which closes itself up and retreats into the silence of the sea.

You can do these exercises in your bedroom (which you should first have aired well) before you go to sleep.

You should go on doing them regularly, night after

night, even if it seems to you that they're doing no good. Yoga exercises are cumulative in their effect, and the advantages are not all felt at once.

Begin, as always, lying on your back, with several minutes of relaxation. And then . . .

1) *The Knee and Nose Posture*

Stretched out on your back in the position of rest, take one of your knees in both hands and draw it down toward your chest.

Breathe out.

Then raise your head and touch your knee with your nose.

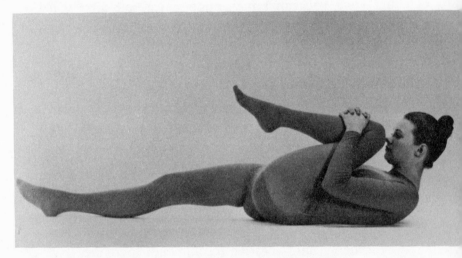

Straighten your leg slowly and lower it to the floor. Do the same exercise using your other leg.

Repeat the complete exercise three times.

2) *The Egg*

Still flat on your back, this time draw both knees toward your chest.

Raise your head.

Breathe out, at the same time resting your forehead against your knees. Return slowly to your original position.

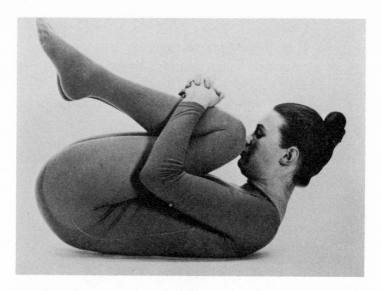

3) *The Rocking Chair*

Sit down and, clasping your knees with both hands, draw them toward your head.

Round your shoulders, dropping your chin toward your chest.

Breathe in and begin to rock yourself backward and forward, as far as you can possibly go.

Do this exercise several times.

The Rocking Chair is not a traditional yoga posture, but an exercise in flexibility. It massages the back, and because it acts on the nerves radiating from the vertebrae, it tends to relax all the organs of the body.

4) *The Fish*

There are several variations on this exercise. You may begin with two of the simplest.

Lying on your back on the floor, bend your knees, part them, and press the soles of your feet together.

Stretch your arms over your head and let them rest, palms upward and parallel to each other, on the floor behind you.

Then, still with your knees parted and your legs bent, cross one foot over the other.

Cross your arms behind your head.

When you get tired, change the position of your feet.

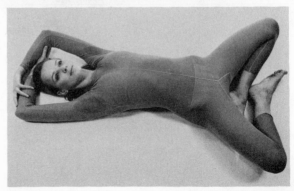

This posture, in both its versions, facilitates freedom of the shoulder and hip joints. But, above all, it "blocks" the rib cage in such a way that you are obliged to practice abdominal breathing, which is, in itself, a powerful relaxing agent.

5) *The Yoga Mudra*

Slowly, without straightening your legs, sit up with the aid of your hands.

Straighten your back.

Take a deep breath, and then lean forward as you breathe out.

Clasp your hands behind your back, keeping your arms flexible, and allow your head to fall forward until it touches the floor.

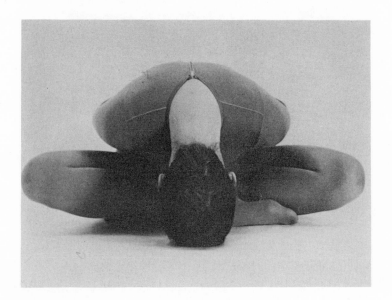

This posture stretches the dorsal muscles and those of the buttocks and the backs of the thighs. It helps to keep the spinal column and the hip and knee joints flexible. It combats constipation and flatulence. And finally, like all the seated postures, it develops your concentration.

6) *The Half-Bridge*

Begin by lying on your back with your knees bent and your feet resting on the floor slightly apart.

Next, arch yourself into the Half-Bridge position, supporting yourself by propping your hips on your hands.

This exercise is done in three stages: First, you breathe in, expanding your stomach. Second, you breathe out, at the same time sucking in your stomach. Third, without breathing in again, you suck in your stomach more and more, as though you were trying to jam it against your backbone.

7) *The Oyster*

Sit down, keeping your back very straight.

Part your knees and draw your feet toward you, sole against sole.

Now widen the angle of the knees into a shallow V shape and lean forward.

Slide your arms under your calves and grasp your ankles.

Breathe out.

Let your head fall forward until it touches your feet.

110

8) *Finish the exercises with a long session of relaxation.*

Yoga can help you to sleep. Don't be satisfied just to take off your clothes when you retire. Mentally get rid of all the other layers that enclose your deepest self.

To start with, strip yourself of your body.

To do this, you must adopt the most comfortable position you can find in bed. The one you usually sleep in is the best.

Once in this position, use the classic relaxation technique: Travel, in thought, all over your body, beginning with your extremities. Sweep aside all the tensions you encounter in your muscles as you go. And finally "let your weight fall."

Imagine that your body has become heavy.

Imagine that it is deeply sunken in the ground, like a ship that has run aground.

Then, gently, leave your body on the bed and transfer your attention to your breathing.

Take several abdominal breaths slowly, and imagine, as you force the air out of your lungs, that you are also forcing out your fatigue.

When your breathing has become calm, peaceful, like that of a sleeping child, you will find yourself at last face to face with the part of you that is most agitated: your mind.

But don't allow yourself to become a slave to your own mind. It has a tendency to pester you, to parade in your memory all the events of the day just ended. It reminds you, obstinately, of all the things you forgot to do, or all the things you have to do tomorrow.

Don't get drawn into this little game!

Remember that it's *your* memory, *your* imagination, *your* dreams that the mind lives on—and refuse to cooperate.

You will find that the images your mind dredges up will dwindle and disappear of their own accord.

After this, stay absolutely immobile, without tension.

After a short time (three to five minutes, usually) you will begin to feel the torpor that steals over you just before sleep.

Soon you will no longer be there to know what happened or how it happened; you will have slid gently into sleep.

You will awaken in the morning—the body rested and prepared, and the heart free—ready to welcome a new day with all it has to bring of uncertainty and of joy.

CHAPTER TWELVE

Yoga without Postures: A Lesson from the Animals

In the streets of Communist China today—more often still in public squares and gardens—the visitors can see a kind of dance performed by children, students, working people, even old men and women. The movements are fluid and gracious, and the dancers seem from a distance to be eddying around the heart of a sphere.

This dance is the famous Tai T'chi T'chuan, the Chinese version of yoga.

Like the Indian variant, T'chuan has been in existence for several thousand years. Like yoga proper, it is a total exercise: It comprises at the same time activity and relaxation, concentration and rest.

But while yoga is composed of certain postures (one assumes a position, holds it for several minutes, and then returns to the position from which he started), T'chuan is essentially mobile. Basically it is a harmony of balances, an alternation of weak and strong tempi; the strong correspond to tensions, and the weak to relaxations. Now the weight is on one foot, now on the other; rarely is it on both at the same time. A raised hand lowers itself and the other hand rises in its turn. No movement ever seems to terminate; each one smoothly transforms itself into its opposite. The beginning is confused with the end without anyone's being able to tell the exact moment when the transition took place.

T'chuan is symbolized by a circle crossed by a wavy line: the Tao. One half of the circle is white. This corresponds to the male principle, the tension, which is the yang. The other half, the yin, corresponds to the female principle, to relaxation, and this half is black. But each half contains a small part of the other, which signifies that everything, at every moment, is ready to transform itself into its opposite.

Yang corresponds to strength, warmth, dryness, the light by which we live, the sun; yin, on the contrary, is identified with flexibility, cold, wetness, the night, and the moon. The Tao symbol thus represents all created things, the alternation of day and night, life and death, summer and winter, happiness and pain. To obey the laws of Tao is to conform to the laws of life itself; it is a guarantee of equilibrium and success.

I always remember my first meeting with the Chinese master Cheng Man Ching. He was then a man of sixty, a diminutive, wrinkled figure in a long black woolen robe and felt slippers. His head was shaved, with the exception of two long locks dangling to his cheeks, and his muscles (which he made me feel) were supple but as hard as steel.

Explaining that the practice of T'chuan had given him "an immortal body," the sage invited me to take up a position facing him. He put his weight on his right foot, the knee slightly bent, the left foot behind, and asked me to do the same. Then he pressed his right forearm against mine and asked me to carry out various movements of advance and retreat (of tension or relaxation) without ever breaking the contact.

"There is no point at all," he told me, "in trying to make a demonstration of strength, or attempting to overthrow your partner. The aim is to work with finesse, so that each movement is worthy of comparison with a thrust in fencing. As your opponent, I must follow every movement you make and oppose it with the flexible resistance of my own body.

"All the secrets of action are in that. You must learn to yield before an adversary—or before adversity —the better to recover afterward; to foresee the movement in time to forestall it.

"If the thrust comes from above, bend down. If it comes from below, stand erect again. If it is quick, answer quickly. If it is expressed gently, reply gently.

"In any case, never flee. Never break the contact. Stick to the action—and stay alert.

"Truth is stubborn. If you follow these precepts— not only in the practice of T'chuan but in your everyday life—you will triumph in the end and overcome all your problems."

Animals, more than men, possess the secret of the right movement at the right time, probably because an animal's psyche is too primitive to interfere with instinctive reactions. At rest, an animal is completely without tension, its muscles totally relaxed, but it needs only a fraction of a second to mobilize its energy. In that instant of time it becomes ready to pounce or to flee.

An animal commands such a reserve of instant energy because it never wastes any. Its muscles have exactly the power necessary to carry out the job required of them.

It was from observations such as these that the Chinese discovered the secrets of T'chuan.

The "right" attitude, Cheng Man Ching taught me, is therefore the one in which we can best control our tensions.

I remember his instructions: "Stand with your legs slightly apart, your feet parallel and your heels separated by the width of your shoulders. You should hold yourself erect, but with a certain flexibility, your knees bent slightly. Your attitude, in fact, should be the opposite of an *en garde* posture.

"Now, raise your arms slowly in front of you, keeping your elbows slightly flexed, until they are at shoulder height. Your hands should be an extension of your arms, your fingers an extension of your palms.

"Breathe in. Slowly lower your arms as you breathe out—but follow through with your gesture without actually letting your arms drop.

"In this 'right' attitude, your arms are never stretched, but are kept slightly bent so that you can control your muscular tension.

"When you are tense, and your muscles contract, you squander your energy; when you are passive but still in a state of contraction, you waste it: It drains from your body. But in this 'right' attitude you retain your energy. If you want to be sure never to lose your energy, you must be vigilant and relaxed at the same time. Your stance should be flexible, your spine supple, your head balanced, with the nape of your neck stretched and your chin slightly tucked in. Your head should be so 'light' that it feels as though it were hanging from the ceiling on a wire.

"Always breathe through your nose. Inhale calmly, deeply, in your natural rhythm—but moving only your diaphragm. Your chest, rib cage, and shoulders should remain relaxed. Only in this way can the breath, which brings energy with it, enter your body unobstructed. Imagine that air is accumulating in your abdomen (at that point a couple of inches from the navel that is the body's center of gravity). Actually, it is the energy of the ether—which the Hindus call prana and the Chinese call ch'i—that is concentrating in your body. You should feel that it is the air that makes your lungs move. You should have the impression that your lungs do not move by themselves: They do not breathe but they *are breathed.*

"Air has a certain density, but we have lost the faculty of *feeling* it. To test the air's 'resistance,' stroke it with your arms as though you were swimming; imagine you are in the water. Your movements will conform naturally to the principles of T'chuan.

"Be calm as the mountain—and mobile as the stream."

This "right" attitude of which the master was speaking is in fact a kind of yoga without postures.

If you adopt it and practice it, you will never be tense, and never too relaxed; you will live in that marginal zone where we remain masters of our own bodies, at the same time aloof, wide awake, aroused, attentive, and intensely *aware.*

CHAPTER THIRTEEN

Where Do You Go from Here?

Right from the beginning of this book (if you happen to be gifted that way), or at any rate during the course of it (if you have worked with the necessary concentration), you have been learning to master your emotions.

Perhaps this wasn't the goal you envisioned when you started. You were probably hoping to control your body and not your emotions; first, because command of your emotions seemed impossible, and second, because the very idea of "mastery" seemed false—one doesn't stop a horse in full gallop.

But then one day you discovered there had been a change in you.

You used to be nervous. You started at sudden noises. You lost control easily, both of your words and your movements. Then suddenly you somehow acquired a certain interior power, a facility for breaking contact so that *you were no longer always being thrown violently into the world of the emotions.*

What is an "emotion" anyway?

It is a complex process that modifies the subtle chemistry of the body. When you are moved, your autonomous nervous system instantly stimulates your suprarenal glands, which secrete adrenaline. The adrenaline is released into your bloodstream, where it accelerates your heartbeat and whips your nervous system into action. Your blood pressure rises, and your blood vessels contract. You are in effect in a vicious circle, because the more you are moved, the more nervous or violent you become. If, however, you can stand aside from it all, you have broken the circle at the start; you have acquired that self-mastery that derives only from a permanent self-transformation. This is completely different from an artificial attitude of disinterest or a simple exterior exercise of control.

You have in fact become a free man or woman: *free at last to be yourself*. This is truly the first meeting you have ever had with your inner self.

Can you go on beyond yoga?

Of course you can. Yoga, don't forget, comes from the East, as does the initial stage of relaxation. If you want to voyage further into self-knowledge, you should look toward India or the Far East, toward Vedanta or Zen Buddhism.

It is not enough, though, simply to read books. Books can never be more than landmarks or guides. They serve to light the way and point out the route to be followed. They will be useless unless you try to *live* them.

Take this book as an example: It will be of little help to you if you just read it, but it can help a great deal if you "do" it. Every time you take one step by learning from books, you must take two more by working hard within yourself to use that knowledge.

How do you go on from here?

First, you must concentrate even more on relaxation; deepen it and make it more intense. The more you progress with these exercises, which seem simple at first, the more you will discover resistances and tensions within you that you never suspected. You will discover that you can always relax just a little bit more;

no matter how far you go, you never reach the end of the road.

Secondly, you must deepen your relationship to the simple things of life, to the earth you walk on, to the manifestations of nature that surround you. You must live by the rhythms of nature and never oppose them: Live by day, sleep by night; eat the fruits and vegetables that are in season; cut down on meat, tobacco, and liquor. You must be alive to your own inner cleanliness, to the direction of your personal ethic.

What will your reward be?

You have already learned how to be an autonomous being, independent of the outside world. Now you will discover the value of silence: silence of the heart, silence of the imagination, silence of the senses and of the memory. "I rediscovered the silence of the body," a yoga adept told me once. "Since then I have lived in a state of euphoria that is like a second childhood, a renewal of youth."

Finally, you will progress to a state in which you are independent in your solitude yet at the same time intensely aware of the world around you.

And if that's not happiness, what is?

Paris, July, 1968

120

Glossary

ATTENTION—Concentration of the mind on a given point. If you are asked to concentrate your attention on your arm, you must will yourself to *feel* the weight of the limb and not allow your thoughts to wander.

AUTOMATISM—Movement, or a series of movements, accomplished mechanically, without the intervention of the will. Dressing yourself, going down a staircase, jumping back from danger—these are examples of automatism.

APNEA (*and* DYSPNEA)—Filling the lungs with air and retaining it there for several seconds voluntarily is termed apnea. Expelling the air, keeping the lungs empty voluntarily is dyspnea.

ASANA—Hindu word signifying "posture." Yoga comprises a series of asanas. You assume a posture slowly; you hold it, without moving, for several seconds; and then you return slowly to your original position.

COMPLEX—Ensemble of unconscious tendencies determining our reactions to a person, an object, or a situation.

CONCENTRATION—Synonym for attention—but with a little bit extra. Attention can be involuntary. It can fluctuate, or pass rapidly from one object to another. But concentration is deliberate and relatively stable. In concentration the attention is voluntarily fixed upon an idea, a sensation, or an object.

CONSCIOUSNESS (*and* UNCONSCIOUSNESS)—Consciousness is the ensemble of ideas and images appearing on the clear screen of the mind. The unconscious comprises all that escapes our consciousness but remains nevertheless a part of us. The psychologist Carl Jung compared the two to an iceberg, the visible portion being the conscious mind, the submerged part the unconscious. Just as the submerged section of the ice, which is much larger in volume and weight, ceaselessly directs the movements of the part we can see, everything that exists in our unconscious influences our conduct.

CONTRACTION (*and* DECONTRACTION)—When you contract a muscle, it swells. The nerve fibers shorten, and the nervous influx into the muscle increases. Decontraction stretches the muscle and diminishes the nervous influx.

CORTEX—Gray matter covering the brain, whose wrinkled and folded surface would cover, stretched out, about two square yards. Only a few millimeters thick, it is the seat of our character.

DISCONNECTION—Cerebral disconnection is like an electrical disconnection: It implies cutting the passage of a current. This means a slowing or an interruption of the flow of messages from the brain, with a consequent absence of the reactions or responses that would normally follow them.

ELECTROMYOGRAPH—Electrical instrument for measuring the tension in a muscle.

ELONGATION—Synonym for stretching. When a muscle works "at force," it swells and shortens, becoming thick and lumpy. When it can work "in elongation," it acquires strength and slenderness.

EMOTION—Intense, brief reaction of the organism to an unexpected situation. Emotion can be agreeable or painful, but manifests itself in either case in disorders of the bodily functions. Emotion can make us short of breath, cover us with perspiration, speed up the heartbeat, and so on.

ENDOCRINE GLANDS—Glands secreting the different hormones necessary for normal body function and the maintenance of good health.

122

EQUILIBRIUM—Physical equilibrium, like psychic equilibrium, is a state of balance that is constantly unstable, and that we must at all times work to correct.

FIELD (*of* CONSCIOUSNESS)—Ensemble of awareness at a given moment.

HORMONES—Substances secreted by the endocrine glands that are indispensable to the proper functioning of the body.

HYPNOSIS—State of partial sleep, artificially induced, in the course of which the subject is capable of obeying certain suggestions made by the hypnotist.

INHIBITION—Diminution or total arrest of a function. For example, when we feel ourselves in danger, we want to run—but fear may paralyze us.

IMAGE (*or* BODY IMAGE)—Mental representation we have of ourselves.

IMAGINATION—Ability to recall mentally objects that are absent and to combine images—in short, our creative gift.

KINESTHERAPY—Science permitting cure of the body by manipulation of the joints and muscles.

MIND—Commands the ensemble of our intellectual operations.

MUSCLES (VOLUNTARY *and* INVOLUNTARY)—Voluntary muscles are those over which we exercise control, those that permit us to raise our arms, walk, sit down, play games, etc. Involuntary muscles are those functioning independently of our will—in the stomach, the intestines, etc.

NERVOUS INFLUX—Language traversing the brain and the nerve fibers. The messages perceived by our senses, the orders we give to our muscles, travel in the form of pulsations or waves of nervous influx.

PALMING—System of resting the eyes by cupping them in the palms of the hands to exclude light.

PITUITARY GLAND—Command post of the endocrine system. The hormones it secretes regulate the function of other endocrine glands.

PSYCHE (PSYCHISM, *etc.*)—The root "psy" derives from the Greek *psyche*, which signifies soul. The term designates that which has no material existence. (See also SOMA.)

REFLEX (CONDITIONED)—An immediate involuntary response to a particular situation.

REPRESSION—Psychological process whereby feelings, memories, or desires that seem impossible to realize are pushed into the unconscious.

SENSITIVITY—Faculty of perceiving impressions received by our own bodies, or from the world around us. Reaction to the messages delivered by our senses or our minds. Can be more or less sharp, more or less refined. We are more or less sensitive to cold, to pain, to wounding words.

SOMA—Employed in the sense of "pertaining to the body," as opposed to that pertaining to the soul, or psyche.

STRESS—Marked reaction of the organism to external or psychic shock.

SUBCONSCIOUS—Zone separating the conscious from the unconscious. Comprises things of which we are only vaguely aware, things we have known but forgotten, things which might, at any moment, return to the memory.

SUGGESTION *and* AUTOSUGGESTION—In suggestion, you submit passively to the influence of thoughts from outside yourself. You accept them without controlling them, or discussing them, as though your willpower had been submerged in that of another. In autosuggestion, you accept that you will submit, passively, to an idea—but with the difference that you have yourself formulated this idea.

TAI T'CHAI T'CHUAN—System of gymnastics practiced for several centuries in China. Employs complementary forces of yin and yang (see below).

TENSION—State of that which is pulled or stretched. All effort, physical, intellectual, or psychic, creates physical or mental tension.

THORAX—Segment of the body formed by the ribs and the organs they protect (heart, liver, lungs, etc.)

124

TONUS—Degree of variable tension in a muscle. Minimum tonus is the tonus of rest. Tonus of attitude is the tonus necessary to keep us on our feet, or balanced. By extension (and analogy) one speaks of intellectual tonus, nervous tonus, psychic tonus, etc.

TRAUMATIC—Pertaining to a shock, bodily or mental, which has left a wound.

YANG *and* YIN—Chinese terms. Yang is the masculine principle, symbolizing all that is strong, warm, bitter, and dry (e.g., the sun). Yin, the female principle, corresponds to whatever is cold, sweet, flexible, and moist (e.g., the moon). For the Chinese and Japanese it is the contest between these forces that constitutes the universe.

YOGA *and* HATHA-YOGA—Hindu words for the ensemble of disciplines, mental and physical, permitting man to bridge the gap separating him from the infinite. Hatha-yoga is one part of these disciplines—that part corresponding especially to the body. In this book the single word yoga can be taken for hatha-yoga throughout.